Entrepreneurship
The Art of Embracing the Unknown

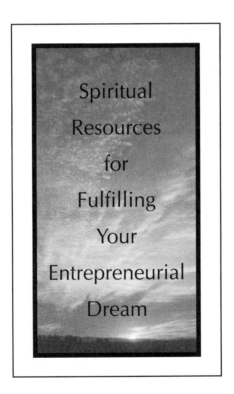

Spiritual Resources for Fulfilling Your Entrepreneurial Dream

Lauren Black Schwarz

For permissions requests, contact the publisher at:
Executive Excellence Publishing
1344 East 1120 South
Provo, UT 84606
phone: 1-801-377-4060
toll free: 1-800-304-9782
fax: 1-801-377-5960
www.eep.com

For Executive Excellence books, magazines and other products, contact Executive Excellence directly. Call 1-800-304-9782, fax 1-801-377-5960, or visit our website at www.eep.com.

Printed in the United States

10 9 8 7 6 5 4 3 2 1

ISBN 1-890009-58-X

Cover design by Ginger McGovern
Printed by Publishers Press

Advance Praise for . . .

Entrepreneurship

The Art of Embracing the Unknown

"Laurie Schwarz has written the 'how to' book of overcoming obstacles and rising above mediocrity. During the early years of Full Sail (now fondly referred to as the Roller Coaster Years), the challenges were sometimes overwhelming. I wish this book had been around then! Bill and Laurie have endured, encouraged, inspired, and smiled their way through many of the same challenges! This book will tell you how they did it, and how their faith and vision can help you make your dreams come true."

—*Jon Phelps, CEO, Full Sail*

"As an entrepreneur, you will inevitably find yourself facing challenges and setbacks that will rob you of your drive and desire. When I invented the Super Soaker™, I had no idea of the difficulties that I would encounter over the ten-year period it took to achieve market success. Periodically, I would stumble upon a morsel of inspiration that I would internalize to rejuvenate my effort. I wish that this book had been available a long time ago, for it is truly a feast that nourishes and sustains the human spirit. It offers a philosophy and perspective of life that will empower you to succeed."

—*Lonnie G. Johnson, President,*
Johnson Research and Development Company, Inc.

"In an uncertain world, you can either flow with the uncertainty, like a cork on top of the water, or hold fast to the past and be buried alive, like a skier caught in an avalanche. This book will teach you to ride the crest and stay buoyant."

—Dr. H. James Harrington, Principal, International Quality Advisor, Ernst and Young, LLP; Author, The Continuous Improvement Process

"Lauren has hit the mark. If we learn to live in the present, let go, balance our lives, and find joy in service, we will not only be better entrepreneurs, we will be more effective, happier people."

—Gary Heil, CEO, The Center for Innovative Leadership; author, Leadership and the Customer Revolution

"With respect to the new millennium, we find more and more people trying to uncover true satisfaction in their lives, often by becoming entrepreneurs; however, we must realize that real answers come from within ourselves. In this book, Laurie Schwarz reveals the essence of being or living with an entrepreneur through poignant examples from her own life. She focuses on the challenges of overcoming the 'turbulent water' and achieving inner strength and purpose. This is a **must read** for every 'caterpillar' who truly wants to be a 'butterfly'!"

—Judy Scherer, Editor, Competitive Edge! magazine

"After you are successful, your entrepreneurial efforts look brilliant, simple, and obvious to everyone. This book is about getting through the rough times when the dream is far from obvious and it looks like there are no answers. For many out there, this book will make the difference between another failure and a fabulous success. It has lots of gold nuggets—practical knowledge you can put to work."

—John M. Segal, President, North American Products, National Advisor Cabinet, Norman Vincent Peale Leadership Center

And I said to the man who stood at the gate of the year: "Give me a light that I may tread safely into the unknown." And he replied: "Go out into the darkness and put your hand into the hand of God. That shall be to you better than a light and safer than a known way."

—Minnie Louise Haskins
English poet, 1875-1957

Dedication

THIS BOOK IS DEDICATED with heartfelt devotion and appreciation to the three loves of my life: Bill, my husband, partner, lover, and friend of thirty years; Vail, my precious, loving, and gifted daughter; and Kord, my joyful, talented, and inspiring son. Without the loving support of each of you, this work would not exist. We are one, and I thank you.

Acknowledgments

LIKE YOU, I AM A PART OF ALL whose lives have touched mine and whose words I have read. It would be impossible to thank them all. For ease of accountability, I am placing the people who have made the greatest contribution to my life in time segments, so that I might remember and acknowledge as many as possible.

My gratitude goes first of all to my birth family. I am particularly indebted to my parents, Stephen A. and Lea Vail Black, for the great spiritual heritage I received from their desire that their children know a loving, personal God who continues to reveal Himself to all who seek to know Him. At the tender age of seven, I made a commitment in the waters of baptism to study and follow to the best of my ability the life and teachings of Jesus the Christ. Despite two dark periods when I strayed from Him, it is my testimony that He never once deserted me. This book is possible only because the Holy Spirit first put it into my mind to write and then remained as a constant source of inspiration.

I am deeply appreciative of my sister, Michele Hays, and her husband Bruce Morton, for extending their love and hospitality, enabling me to meet my business and personal obligations. With the use of their beautiful mountain home in Stowe, Vermont, I had the uninterrupted writing time necessary to complete this book.

I am grateful to my sister-in-law, Judith Schwarz, for the caretaking she provides for our pets and home, allowing me to devote my time to my speaking, writing, and consulting work.

Many dear friends have contributed to this manuscript either by allowing me to interview them and tell their stories or by reading it and giving me editorial assistance or feedback. These include Hugh and Lynda Adamson, Joan Ashford, Dot Blum, Susan Carey, Dana Denton, Jan Flint, Peter Grant, Lynda Hill, Marie Kane, Don Kremer,

Polly Miller, Sterling Nelson, Nina Soler Reid, Kathryn Rubick, Jon and Esther Phelps, Trent Price, Cheri Scott, Sara and John Segal, Pam Shelton, Faye Smith, Judy Schalick, Linda Vephula, Jim Vallanueva, Nicola Whistler, and Sally Wilson. A special thanks to my Executive Excellence Publishing team. I love each of you, and I thank you for the generous gift of your belief, time, and support.

Learning Laboratories

As the co-founder of Learning Laboratories, Inc., I had the unique opportunity to personally meet and learn from the following brilliant and generous people; their writings and philosophies are a part of whom I am today: Albert Ellis, Ph.D., Rational Emotive Therapy; Willard Fey, Ph.D.; William Glasser, Ph.D., Reality Therapy; Thomas Gordon, Ph.D., Parent Effectiveness Training; Thomas Harris, M.D., Transactional Analysis; Eugene Jennings, Ph.D., Executive Stress; Dorothy Jongeward, M.Ed., Transactional Analysis; Ralph Nichols, Ph.D., Effective Listening; George Odiorne, Ph.D., Management by Objectives; Paul Hersey, Ph.D., Situational Leadership; Sid Simon, Ph.D., Values Clarification; Jack Gibb, Ph.D., Creating Communities Based on Trust; Kenneth Cooper, M.D., Aerobic Health; Harvey Jackins, Re-Evaluation Counseling; Otis Maxfield, Ph.D., Jungian Psychology; David W. Merrill, Ph.D., The Social Style Profile; M. Scott Myers, Ph.D., Job Enrichment; Gordon L. Lippitt, Ph.D., Organizational Renewal; William V. Haney, Ph.D., Communications and Perception; Robert Shaw, Ph.D., Contextual Therapy; Gerard I. Nierenberg, The Art of Negotiating; Cody Sweet, Ph.D., Body Language; Robert Tannebaum, Ph.D., Leadership.

I also wish to thank the thousands of Learning Laboratories' students, as well as the business and personal clients who, over a period of many years, trusted their personal and corporate development to our care. Each of you contributed to our lives by the depth of your sharing and willingness to be vulnerable as we discovered together the principles, concepts, and tools that accelerated individual and organizational transformation.

The Corporate Satellite Television Network, Inc. (CSTN)

The moment Bill and I stepped out in faith to establish CSTN, people caught the vision. The dream could not have become a reality without those who readily joined forces with us by lending their friendship, time, talents, money, and other resources. We are eternally grateful to the following staff and personal support team:

Phase One: Joan and Jim Channon, Creative Video, Joel Cowan, Jerry Gardner, Lois Guilbeau, Dr. Jay Hammer, Patrick Mars, Susan Mewborn, Walter and Susan Snead, Richard Rex and Dixieland Productions, Jerry Schmidt, Kay Timmons and Nations Bank, Dale and Pamela Truax.

Phase Two: Nick Ashton, Richard Bowers, Blaine Colton and Keystone Communications, Tyler Clements, Robert Crowe, Jan Flint, Newt Gingrich, Tom Ledford, David Miller, Jon and Esther Phelps, Randy Rivers, Sally Safford, GTE Spacenet, Michael Summerford, Bruce A. Taylor, Harrison Taylor, Linda Vephula, Cindy Ehmers, and Jack Murray.

The Faculty: Kenneth Blanchard, Ph.D.; Marjorie Blanchard, Ph.D.; Hyler Bracey; Martin Broadwell; Tony Buzan; William R. "Max" Carey, Jr.; Ram Charan; Stephen R. Covey, Ph.D.; Harvey Coleman; Charles A. Coonradt; Thomas Crum; Dave Garwood; H. James Harrington, Ph.D.; Gary M. Heil; Ned Herrmann, Ph.D.; John E. Jones, Ph.D.; J. Clayton Lafferty, Ph.D.; George Land, Ph.D.; Lawrence M. Miller; Esther Orioli; Richard (Rick) W. Tate; and Larry Wilson.

Affiliates, Friends, and Supporters: Norman Bodek; Bill Brooks; Betsy and Rich Brown; BJ, Jim and Michael Chikiris; Peggy and Ron Condon; Ron and Eva Currens; Larry Dennis; Tricia Euen; B. Ray Helton; Davina A. Henderson; Bryant Hodgson; Angela Holland; Janet Julian; Diane and Don Kremer; Tom Noon; Marie Oberle;

Merrill Oster; Pat Portway; John Roberts; Dr. Robert Robideau; Sara and John Segal; John Sperling; Jack Wilder; and Ed Yager.

The Learning Organization and The CEO Alliance

Wes Cantrell, CEO, Lanier Worldwide; Dennis P. Cronin, Co-Founder, The CEO Alliance; Tom Foss, CEO, Hill & Foss, Inc.; Terry A. Hill, CEO, Applied Business Corporation; Roy Miller, CEO, Southern Packaging Machinery; Bud Mingledorff, CEO, Mingledorff's; Dave Shepherd and The Atlanta Athletic Club; Jeff Snow, CEO, HiFi Buys; Jim Thompson, CEO, Thomco Specialty Products, Inc.; Jim Villanueva, CEO, Kieffer Paper & Pulp Mills; Norman Vincent Peale, Executive Leadership Conference.

Contents

Foreword 13

Introduction..23

CHAPTER 1: Focusing on Your Vision and Values 29
Out of our entrepreneurial vision, we learn
to focus on the big picture, to clarify our
values, and to keep our perspective.

CHAPTER 2: Determining Your Personal Purpose 45
By clearly seeing our personal purpose, we
make setbacks into events that help us
achieve our purpose and our vision.

CHAPTER 3: Experiencing the Joy of Service......................55
When we get outside our narrow focus on
self, we experience firsthand the joyful role
of the leader as servant.

CHAPTER 4: Committing to Commitment 71
By learning to keep our word, we discover
the power of personal commitment and how
Providence then helps us fulfill our vision.

CHAPTER 5: Seeing Everything as a Resource 83
When things look the most grim, we learn
to step out in faith and to see resources all
around us that were there all along.

CHAPTER 6:   Learning to Let Go **95**

   We find that what we try to control will
   control us, so we detach ourselves and
   control only ourselves and our responses.

CHAPTER 7:   Living in the Present **117**

   By charting events in our lives over time, we
   shed the limited social roles and images that
   we hide behind in our models of reality.

CHAPTER 8:   Consciously Creating What You Want..........**145**

   We learn to conceive, choose, and experience our goals by using structural tension
   and the tools and power of creative thought.

CHAPTER 9:   Developing Perspective and Life Balance **161**

   By developing perspective and humor, we
   gain a clear understanding of what's truly
   important, becoming stewards of our health.

CHAPTER 10: Doing unto Others **179**

   We learn about Senior Forces of Change, give
   others what we want, establish trust, build
   partnerships, and make clients of prospects.

CHAPTER 11: Trusting in God **197**

   We master uncertainty and unknowns through
   faith, finding deeper levels of clarity, courage,
   and meaning in all that we do.

CHAPTER 12: Correcting, Completing—and Celebrating! **215**

   Through feedback, we make corrections,
   achieve completions, and enjoy celebrations—
   for every completion deserves a celebration!

Foreword

by Wm. R. 'Max' Carey, Jr.

IN APRIL 1981, I DECIDED TO embrace the unknown, to reach out into that dark, undefined space called entrepreneurship— I decided to start my own business.

Now, it's not as if I hadn't done risky or dangerous things before. For starters, I was born in Queens, New York—that's a pretty risky exercise. I played football in high school, and in college was a punt- and kick-returner and defensive half-back, despite being the smallest player on the team and playing for the losingest team in the league. To add a little more danger and risk to my life, as a Naval carrier- based fighter pilot I flew 100 missions over North Vietnam, earning Top Gun certification. Being lucky enough to return home, I then taught advanced flight training to Navy pilots.

Later as a civilian, I competed daily in one of the most demand- ing entrepreneurial companies in the country—a company that was then known as Pat Ryan & Associates and is now known as AON. It was the second largest insurance brokerage in the world, founded and led by the extraordinarily gifted and charismatic entrepreneurial leader, Patrick G. Ryan.

Little did I know how my experiences up to then would pale com- pared to my "embracing the unknown" experience as an entrepreneur. I wish I could have had Lauren's book back then and could have been braced to meet the unknown of entrepreneuring. Now, some 18 years and many battle scars and invaluable lessons later, there are those who call me "a very successful entrepreneur." What they mean is that, if you compared all the entrepreneurs in the country, I would be in the top 10

13

percent in that group in terms of my success and my understanding and accomplishments. Because of this, I have the opportunity to speak to entrepreneurial audiences, often under the sponsorship of groups like *Inc.* magazine, TEC (The Executive Committee), YPO (Young Presidents Organization), and various Chambers of Commerce.

In first-tier business schools, I have had the opportunity to address pre-entrepreneurial people—those seriously considering going into business for themselves, or what I call "taking the entrepreneurial plunge." It is a truly wonderful experience, but highly predictable. Let me play it out for you, give you a sample of what one of those speeches is like.

After a rousing introduction of my entrepreneurial credentials, I start talking and lead up to my first power questions: How do you become an entrepreneur? As many as 1,000 hands will go up. Everybody has an answer to this question. I call on someone, and they say, "You get an idea." I respond, "Great, you're right on. The first step toward becoming an entrepreneur is to get a good idea. What's the second step?" All the hands go up again. This one they are sure they have. I call on someone and their answer is, "You quit your job."

Here is where I begin to take issue with their responses. I say something like, "Well, we have a slight semantics problem here. Because, when you quit your job, you don't become an entrepreneur. When you quit your job, you become (and I pause there for dramatic effect, and they fill in the blank for me as it starts to reveal itself)— when you quit your job, you become—that's right—unemployed."

There are vast differences between the two. When you quit your job, you become unemployed. Entrepreneurship is the art of becoming gainfully re-employed in your own business. It took me exactly 90 seconds to become unemployed, to say, "I quit," to my employer. It took me years to become an entrepreneur!

I ask another question, "How many of you have ever been unemployed?" And they will look around at each other. Now, these are all people that generally are high achievers, generally have been in control of their own destinies, and generally have always been able to find work of some kind when they needed it: work such as a child working in fast food or as an adult switching jobs or even finding or outsourcing independent contracting work or project work to fill the void or the gap between major career positions.

"How many of you have ever been—or really ever been—unemployed? That means not having a job and not having money coming in." And they all shake their heads, "No." I go on, "Okay, so if you've never had that experience, let me ask you something: Have you ever taken a course on how to be unemployed? Have you ever gone to a seminar on how to be unemployed? Have you ever read a book on how to be unemployed? What to expect? How to act? How to feel, what to do, where to go, who to talk to? So to set this thing in proper perspective, what you are preparing to do when you become an entrepreneur is to do the least sensible thing you've ever done, which is to engage in an activity that will lead you to a predictable outcome, a predictable conclusion—and that is: a) something you've never done before, and b) something you are totally unprepared for because when you start a business you are not prepared to be unemployed.

"You are embarking on a path with a logical short-term destination as a place you have never been and for which you have absolutely no preparation whatsoever. Unemployment. Let's say it another way—no money. How interesting. And people wonder why it is so tough, why it is, indeed, the Unknown!"

In April 1981, I loaded my family, my wife and three little children, into an Oldsmobile V6 wagon and drove to Atlanta, Georgia, to set up my business to become an entrepreneur—company name, Corporate Resource Development. We were going to be the best sales training company in the country. I set the business up in April. I leased 3,000 square feet of custom-designed office space with inlaid rugs, new furniture, pictures, and even a staff of six people. By December, the gas and water had been turned off in my home, and in January 1982, just one month later, my dear sweet wife, Susan, was at the mailbox at the end of the driveway with a neighbor at noontime to collect the mail when a tow truck arrived, and the driver said, "Excuse me, are you Susan

Carey?" She answered, "Yes," and they promptly backed the tow truck into the driveway and repossessed her car.

When I came home that evening and saw the empty garage and the place where Susan's car should have been, you can imagine how awful I felt. How insufficient I felt. How sad I felt. How frightened I felt. I came in and looked at my wife and said, "Susan, was there any way for you to salvage any self-respect in front of that very gossipy neighbor of ours?" And she said, "Oh yes, I handled that for us, Max. I just said, 'Oh that Max, what a funster—always having surprise repairs done on my car!'" Now, have you ever seen cars being repossessed? Give me a break! But I will forever love her for that statement.

When the business goes bad financially—the family goes bad financially. I soon had Atlanta's largest and most accurate list of restaurants that did not have electronic credit check machines. I was their best customer for very short periods of time. Now, don't get me wrong here—don't misunderstand me. I'm not implying to you that I didn't pay my bills. I always paid my bills. In fact, when I started this business, we had never been late on a payment. And to this day, we have never not paid anyone everything we owed them. We were just paying more slowly than American Express would have liked.

That night I took my wife out to dinner on my already discredited American Express card. After a beautiful and well-deserved dinner, I gave the waiter my American Express card. He returned, accompanied by the manager, who told me that he was instructed by American Express to retain my card. All I could think about was the business trip I was taking the next morning that would not be possible without that card. Seeing the corner of my American Express card jutting out of the manager's hand, I told Susan to run get our coats. While she did, I grappled with the manager and managed to disentangle the card from his fingers. We ran out the door and down the street to our car, with the shouts of the manager, "I'm going to call the police!" ringing in our ears.

On the way home that night, I was in deep distress, as you might imagine. I found myself pulling off the road into a state park and driving down by the river. We got out and started walking and talking. I suddenly started making a full disclosure to my wife—completely unplanned and unrehearsed. I opened my heart and started apologizing to her for the situation that I had placed our family in.

As a military man and as a strong performer in a fast-growing entrepreneurial company, I had been a great provider. I had been very predictable and very stable in that regard. Then one day I traded that security for this morass—that is the only way I can describe it, this black hole of tar that I found us in—the black tar of my frailty, my inability to make this company work. And that black tar was touching everything in our lives and sticking to it. My fear was that it was marking it indelibly.

So I apologized to my wife. And as I was apologizing, a realization came to me. The realization was, believe it or not (and it may be difficult for you to believe what I am going to tell you), that, despite how important this business—our livelihood—was to me, my family, and my employees, I had not been giving it everything I had. That I was not applying myself fully to this exercise.

You say that's incredible—it's the most important thing in your world, you would think you would be giving it everything—and, actually, I thought I was until that night, when I suddenly realized I was holding something back.

Today, I think I can rationalize why I did that and why you might be prone to do the same thing. Because if I hold something back, hold back a little, then if I do fail, what can I say, what's my out? I didn't give it everything—it wasn't that important to me. I didn't give it everything I had. So, yeah, it didn't work out. But if I had tried harder, it would have worked out—because Max Carey doesn't fail!

When you commit everything and you announce that you commit everything, then all the rules change. I told my wife that I just realized I wasn't committing everything and that, as of that evening, my pledge to her was that I was going to commit everything. And I know I was truthful. I told her I didn't know if we could keep the doors open. I didn't know if we were going to make it. We were in terrible shape. But my commitment was that from this point forward, she would know that I was giving it everything I had, and if we did not make it, we would know two things: Number One, that I had given it everything and, Number Two, Max Carey was not good enough. And we would have to learn to live with that. Then another amazing thing happened, a very spiritual thing. I started thinking about goals. I realized I had been thinking about the negative, thinking about the downside. So let's think about the positive. Let's think about where this thing could be.

I have a favorite comment from a very dear friend of mine, one of my wingmen from Vietnam, Pat Moneymaker. After a major setback when I needed some solace and uplifting, I had the occasion to talk with Pat. He had this to say to me, "Well, Max, you've had a setback," he said. "But remember the rule: When one door closes, another door opens. Look for the gift. There is always a gift. Find the gift!"

That has become a guiding principle of my life—find the gift. Whenever I have a setback and one door closes, I know that another door opens, and I find the gift. All of a sudden, I am finding a gift. Here's the gift: If this is where we are, then the thing we need to do is to set a really wonderful goal, something we can get excited about—in fact, a goal so good that it is worthy of the pain we are going through right now. If you are in a lot of pain, my advice to you is to set a great goal.

At about that time, I heard about something called the Inc. 500, which is a way of rewarding the fastest growing 500 privately owned companies in America every year, based simply on percentage growth. I had just met a CEO who had received the award, and he was so jubilant that I was really touched by it. I said to Susan, "Why don't we set a goal to make the Inc. 500?" (Now, we did this not even knowing if we would be in business 30 days from that point, but we set the goal anyway.)

Thus we found two gifts: the goal, and the fact that we did it as a team. We had done things together before, but this may have been the first thing we committed as a team. That was the gift. And to add value to that gift, this was the beginning of a new relationship for us because, for the first time in my life, I needed her more than any other person in the world. Sure, I had friends, but I needed her. I needed her to be on this team with me. I needed her to share the dream with me. I needed us to be a team.

Now, I can tell you that something changed that night. I hit the streets the next day, and something was different. Not only did I feel different, not only did I have more enthusiasm and focus and intensity, but people could sense it immediately. They could see it in me. I don't know whether it was through the windows of the soul—in my eyes—or in my step or in my body language, but they knew that I was on my way to doing something special. All of a sudden, things changed. I don't mean to say that it was an overnight turnaround or that it became easy. It never became easy. It became doable, but never easy. However, I could see the light at the end of the tunnel.

With this history in mind, you can imagine how exciting it was for Susan and me to be notified some five years later that we had made the Inc. 500, that we had been selected as one of those companies. Can you imagine?

(After the conference, we realized that we heard something we had never heard before—it was the first time that anyone had ever told us that starting a business was a good idea. It was the first time that anybody had exonerated us or validated our decision. Prior to that day, everybody I talked to told me that I was a nut, that I was a fool, that I was putting my family at risk, that I gave up a good career, and that truly no good things would happen to me along the way. But all of a sudden someone was saying, "Bravo! Mazel Tov! You did something great, and you did it well!"—now, that was a gift!)

So we get to the conference. They are giving out the awards, and I go up to the podium and Wilson Harrell is there. He is an inveterate and consumate entrepreneur, a gentleman who, at a very young age, bought the rights to a bankrupt cleaning product for $35,000—and he launched it in head-to-head competition with the cleaning giants of the day, Mr. Clean and Spic and Span. He did it so successfully that he put them in the back seat and became a market leader. The product was Formula 409. Wilson, by the way, was the first person to engage the services of a TV personaltiy to market a consumer product. He engaged

Art Linkletter as a spokesperson for Formula 409. And because of Art's relationship with children and families, women listened to Art Linkletter, making Wilson's product a household word.

Anyway, I'm at the podium with Wilson Harrell, a swashbuckling, charismatic fellow, and he asks me, "Max, before I give you the award, I would like to ask you a question. I understand that your business climb, your entrepreneurial climb, has been quite painful. Is that not correct?" I answered, "Yes, I have really taken some knocks along the way." He agreed and then asked, "Would it be fair to say, then, that you have a pretty good handle on what people call entrepreneurial terror?" I agreed with him, and he continued, "But we also know that you had another career previous to that. You were a combat flier in Vietnam, completed some 100 missions over North Vietnam in a single-seat jet fighter. So you would know combat terror intimately, too." Again, I agreed with him heartily. He continued, "Max, you have experienced two of life's greatest potential terrors—entrepreneurial terror and combat terror—so I'm sure on the tip of everyone's tongue here is the same question: Of those two great terrors, which was the worst for you?"

It was a great question and, being caught off guard, I was overwhelmed in trying to answer it. I told him I would like to answer it, but to make sure I answered it correctly, I asked him to give me more time. He kindly acquiesced but told me not to forget.

I put some serious thought into it and answered that question in an article that was published in Inc. magazine called "The Superman Complex" (soon to be published as a book). Quoting directly from that article: "Coming home without a paycheck for the first time was far more destructive to me than trying to avoid my first surface-to-air missile in a combat mission into Hanoi at night. After all, it hadn't been my fault that the guy on the ground was shooting at me. He was just doing his job. But it was my fault that I couldn't bring money home to my family. When you are the provider, and you have to walk in and you have to look at your family eyeball-to-eyeball, with no money, you haven't done your job. I just couldn't handle it. And so for me the answer was clear—at least for one man, Max Carey, entrepreneurial terror exceeds combat terror."

Now, people were incredulous when they heard that, and you may be, too. So let me quote another of the paragraphs from that article, in justification: "This fear of failure, this fear of being broke, of not bringing home a proper paycheck for me was constant. When I was in combat, the terror I felt was instantaneous. I'm in an airplane over somebody else's country. They shoot a missile. I turn to beat it. And I avoid it. It explodes as it passes by. I look around, I'm okay. I proceed to target, drop my bombs. I return to ship. I have a hot meal. I sleep in a warm bed. That gut-wrenching terror is over for the day. For 12 hours I have peace. But not so this entrepreneurial fear—not so. This fear was always present, always with me—24 hours a day, seven days a week. And so oppressive and so fearsome, it was like a giant tidal wave that was right behind me, growing ever bigger and moving ever faster. So fearsome, in fact, that I felt that if I paused and turned even long enough to look at it and take its measure, it would inundate me and take me away. So I just kept running."

Entrepreneurship has become the crucible of my life. It's where my greatest adult learning experiences have taken place. Entrepreneurship made my wife and me a team. It made our family a team and filled us with richness. In the sharing of both joys and pain, it has given my family a special characteristic of love, and a special appreciation of the love of God and the role that He plays in our daily lives and ultimate success.

So my advice to you is this: If you want to become an entrepreneur and you want to embrace the unknown that goes with that, read on. This is the handbook for success for the inner spirit and the outer spirit of the entrepreneurial organization and family.

Introduction

ALL OF LIFE IS UNCERTAIN.
Uncertainty is the one common
denominator that touches each
of us at every age, in all economic brackets, in all cultures. The
reflections of Dr. Joshua Loth
Liebman over 50 years ago to his
millions of radio listeners ring as
true today as they did then: "This
is a dangerous world in which to
live, and no normal person can

> Man's greatest triumph
> is to achieve stability
> and inner repose in a
> world of shifting threats
> and terrifying change.
>
> —Bertrand Russell
> *A Free Man's Worship*

face life without experiencing countless fears and worries. They are
part of the fee we pay for citizenship in an unpredictable universe."

When I recently pulled Rabbi Joshua Liebman's *Peace of Mind*
from a shelf in my home library, I was amazed to discover that the
book, published in 1946 and written for "this age of fierce turmoil
and harrowing doubts," was an attempt to find "new answers to the
basic problems of human nature: its needs, motives, fears, and
dreams." In it, the author wrote passionately of his conviction "that
our much-heralded society of security will remain a Utopian vision as
long as the individuals composing that society are desperately insecure, not only economically but emotionally and spiritually." He
went on to say he believed that the crucial problems that presented
themselves in every society would continue.

Today's Headlines of Uncertainty

A glance at today's headline stories reveals the fierce turmoil and harrowing doubts that confront each of us at an ever-accelerating pace.

• Natural disasters of all kinds occur with greater frequency and violence, destroying lives and spreading debilitating destruction.

• Bankruptcy abounds, despite the strongest economy in decades.

• Ninety-five percent of the American economy and new job creation is based on or produced by entrepreneurial businesses. Not one has a safety net, and only a small percent ever survives.

• Corporate cutbacks and layoffs thrust even the most secure adult into fearful insecurity.

• Many who are employed live from paycheck to paycheck or go from job to job, finding high levels of frustration and little satisfaction. Others are tied by "golden handcuffs" to jobs they don't love but are afraid to lose.

• Illness and disease touch each of us, despite accelerated breakthroughs in medical research and technology. The dwindling effectiveness of antibiotics is contributing to alarming health problems in every corner of the globe.

• Children kill each other in fits of rage. Legislators debate whether teachers should be required to carry guns at school. Our concern is no longer just the quality of education but the safety of our children. We pray they will survive elementary and middle school drug free.

• The suicide rate for young people is frighteningly high. The ever-present danger of contracting AIDS or other sexually transmitted diseases continues to haunt them. High school graduation without teen pregnancy is considered a miracle.

• Potentially the biggest problem the modern world has ever faced will likely occur at midnight on January 1, 2000, when most of the world's mainframe and desktop computers (which have been programmed to recognize 2000 as 1900) will either shut down or begin spewing out bad data.

Achieving Stability and Inner Repose in an Uncertain World

No one escapes misfortune. Within every collective tragedy, there lurk individual tragedies. Every house on the block in every neighborhood, city, and country is fraught with private dramas daily. What we require—when facing the unknown in any form—is the ability to see beyond the form and hold life in its proper context. We need to be certain what we can rely on and where we can implicitly place our trust. In other words:

If uncertainty is all there is—is it not our only certainty? In a world where we "win some and lose some," how do we get to a place where we experience winning and losing as one and the same? How do we learn to live in the faith and wisdom of uncertainty? How, when things aren't going our way, do we develop the trust that a reason and purpose much grander than we could ever conceive is at work? How does our reference point become our inner experience, independent of external trappings or the approval and validation of others? How do we create the joy in life as it unfolds before us, hour by hour, day by day?

Out of these issues arises a need to know, a need to learn and master those things that are unfailing in their reliability. Even in a world of change, there are still some basic truths that don't change. These are the fundamental Laws of Life—specific, unchanging success principles for financial, emotional, and spiritual balance that draw into our life whatever we deeply desire. These principles, when internalized and lived, provide a base from which we can operate regardless of our circumstances. They empower us to develop skillful practices and actions for dealing with difficult conditions, people, and situations. Together, they enable us to rise above and master any challenge life throws our way.

My guess is that many of you are already involved in an entrepreneurial venture. Others of you may be dreaming of, or are already on the verge of, starting your own business. In either case, the principles, hands-on tools, and examples in this book can serve as proven, step-by-step guidelines for staying the course as you venture into the unknown.

When you apply the principles and practices from each chapter and make them a part of your everyday living, they will enable you to:

- Develop emotional and spiritual stability
- Live purposely out of your values and vision of what can be
- Put the power of creative thought into action
- Discover and tap into an abundance of resources
- Live from commitment through the power of your word
- Recognize that your current reality is not fixed—because you are the one who created it, and you are the one who can change it

As an entrepreneurial business partner, wife and mother, I can tell you that few lifestyles present a greater challenge in learning to embrace the unknown! By definition, an entrepreneur is someone who lives in a world of uncertainty, with high risk and no guarantees, in order to follow a dream. Whatever your background or life's course, you likely will identify with several of my own real-life situations. (Incidentally, each of these occurred after the age of 45, when my life seemed relatively predictable and financially secure.)

From Caterpillar to Butterfly

My daughter, Vail, has a favorite story from childhood called Hope for the Flowers by Trina Paulus. In this lovely allegory, the author weaves a tale of two caterpillars: Stripe, who has a hard time believing there could be a butterfly inside a fuzzy worm, and Yellow, who aids him in the search for meaning and purpose in life by showing him who he truly is.

The change that occurs in the life cycle of a butterfly is probably the most striking example of metamorphosis. Just as the transformation of the caterpillar into a butterfly begins with a surrender to the unknown, we, too, must let go of what we cling to, realizing that whatever we hold on to is holding us back.

Although we are unable to foresee God's great design for our own purposeful change, within the cocoon of our own lives a transformation is also taking place. Embracing the unknown is like the chrysalis stage within the cocoon of a butterfly, requiring us to wrap ourselves in our own blankets of faith, love, and protection, realizing that we, too, are part of a much greater mission and destiny that is often beyond our comprehension.

My hope for you, the reader, is that this book will provide a cocoon-like resource to comfort and sustain you through your own times of darkness, pain, and uncertainty, and that it will enable you to let go of whatever it is you cling to that no longer serves your highest good.

Unlike the caterpillar, you and I tend to neglect and distrust our own instincts. We seldom allow our inner guidance to get us through the dim parts of life. But, like the caterpillar, you and I have been given everything we need to bring ourselves back into the light and fulfill our own destiny—as this book, hopefully, makes clear. No matter how dark the journey through your own transformation process may seem, the cocoon will not fail to provide the sustenance for a powerfully transformed life.

Chapter 1

Focusing on Your Vision and Values

He who cherishes a beautiful vision, a lofty ideal in his heart, will one day realize it. . . . Your vision is the promise of what you shall one day be.

—James Allen, *As a Man Thinketh*

To see things in the seed. That is genius.

—Lao Tsze, teacher of Confucius

LIFE PRINCIPLE:

Focus determines results.

Above all else, guard your heart, for it is the wellspring of life.

—King Solomon, Proverbs 4:23

IF YOU ARE AN ENTREPRENEUR, or are living with one, you know how exhilarating and contagious the pursuit of a dream can be. You may also have experienced the downside: frustration, desperation, and loneliness. For the less initiated, I think it is fair to compare entrepreneurial living to a roller coaster ride.

For some people, riding on a roller coaster is a bit more adventure than they care to experience. Most of us, however, board a roller coaster feeling relatively safe and somewhat excited. We know, barring some unlikely technical malfunction, that we are at minimal risk. We rely on the seat belt and guardrail to hold us in the car, and trust that the centripetal force generated will keep the cars on the track. Some folks (like my children) will even let go of the bar and ride with both hands in the air for an added thrill.

If you can picture a roller coaster without a guard rail going full speed—and then imagine it suddenly without seat belts—you will have a good idea what the entrepreneurial life can be like. One minute you can be sailing along, enjoying the hills and valleys of the ride. Then suddenly, your relatively stable life can take some terrifyingly sharp dips and turns. You may find yourselves clutching the sides of the car and each other, eyes tightly shut, praying for a safe recovery. And you will consistently need to remind yourself to breathe.

I suspect that all of us at some time or another find ourselves racing headlong down the track of life feeling frightened, vulnerable, and out of control. In the process of surviving the ride, you too may have to gather all your faith and courage, focus your vision, and continuously remind yourself why you got on board in the first place.

Focusing on the Big Picture

To survive any overwhelming situation or wrenching change, we must continuously clarify our vision and focus on the Big Picture. Successful entrepreneurs are not merely dreamers. They are people with vision, the ability to see something not yet materialized. To make any dream a reality, you must first hold a clear picture of it in your heart and mind. By holding true to your vision, you activate the principle that whatever one feels deeply and visualizes clearly will sooner or later materialize.

Envisioning is a creative process that clarifies, crystallizes, and affirms your inner convictions, opening the way for their realization. For me, it is like having a light in my mind that beams just ahead, allowing me to see the next step in writing this book. Our friend, Dr. Kenneth Blanchard, puts it this way: "A vision is a guiding light to live by, 365 days a year. It is the reason you go to work and the reason your organization exists. A real vision gets tucked away in the mind, not the drawer; it shapes every thought and decision. At the same time, a vision is a spiritual statement of one's relation to God and the rest of humanity. It is this very quality that makes it so relevant to our day-to-day experience; a true vision is a blueprint for daily action."

Where we place our focus is one of the few things we have absolute control over. Vision and clarity of focus are tremendous sources of power. In the words of world-famous golfer/entrepreneur Jack Nicklaus, "Vision gives me a line to the cup just as clearly as if it's tattooed on my brain." What we focus on determines the results we produce. It's one of the guiding principles of life.

Vision works both consciously and unconsciously to produce specific results in our lives. Whether we are worrying, judging, and struggling—or acting from commitment and inspiration—the process is still at work. The ultimate key to utilizing vision is to look at the results you have already produced around you. These will either validate the underlying principles you are successfully applying or reveal to you the principles being violated. Vision also allows you to view turmoil or setbacks as pertinent feedback, indicating the need for correction.

Context Determines Content

It is impossible to manage a life of ambiguity without firmly establishing the context of what is going on.

Context has to do with perspective—the way you hold, frame, or view something (an experience, idea, or function). It is the larger setting or deeper meaning behind a word or phrase, relating to the entire situation, background, or environment. Perspective creates thoughts, and thoughts create experience. Since your experience of life depends on your perspective, your ability to see life contextually is one of the most valuable qualities you can possess. As you master context, you free yourself from the content, or form, of your life.

Acknowledging the Way Things Are

As humans, we are able to deal with almost anything—as long as we know what we are dealing with. That is why the truth sets you free. When you understand the way things are, you know what to expect and what is expected of you. It is the uncertainty, the not knowing, that can make life crazy.

For instance, many people are not accustomed to discussing business or financial matters with their families. It is just not something they talk about. Perhaps they don't want to worry their spouse or upset their children. But I believe that young people can always tell when something is wrong. They tend to internalize situations because they do not have the life experience to evaluate and solve problems. I know of a situation where the parents were quite distressed about not being able to make an insurance payment, but didn't reveal what was wrong. By misinterpreting the upset, their children thought something tragic had happened that they were not being told about, and they became unduly worried. In retrospect, it wasn't tragic, although it was unnerving and cause for concern. By simply telling the truth about the cause for concern and the expected outcome, a great deal of unnecessary worry could have been avoided.

When our family lost all forms of insurance for several years, we knew that was the way things were at the time, so everyone knew to use caution and to take good care of themselves. When our son Kord broke his nose during a friendly neighborhood basketball game, he automatically knew we wouldn't be able to have a plastic surgeon fix it right away.

The life of a friend of mine, Sally, was thrown into upheaval when her husband, Jim, left a successful law practice to become a mid-life entrepreneur. After he achieved astounding success in real estate, the market hit a huge slump, and they suddenly lost almost everything. While helping Sally establish a context for what was happening in their lives, I asked, "How much do the girls know of everything that's going on?"

"We've not yet sat down to talk with them, and I am afraid they're getting a distorted view of things, like why mom's tense and upset. I'm concerned they may think it has to do with them, or that it's our marriage that's not right."

"That's easy to do," I replied.

"I was thinking I'd talk with them about the phase our life is in right now with Jim gone so much. Kids understand phases because they go through them all the time. We want them to understand that they're going to be fine, even though it's a lean time, and they're not used to that. Their wants won't always be met—but their needs will be."

Encouraging her to do this, I suggested, "Perhaps some sort of analogy would help."

Sally brightened and responded, "Well, it's football season. I could explain how it's half-time in our lives right now. We're going into the third and fourth quarters. We're behind and have to catch up. We don't quite know how we're going to do that or what the final score will be because we've had a big fumble on the goal line. But the game's not over."

"Sally, that's wonderful! Why don't you encourage them to be family cheerleaders?"

Staying Focused—Regardless of the Circumstances

As the children of entrepreneurs, Kord and our daughter, Vail, grew up experiencing both privilege and deprivation. Their early years were rather idyllic. While they were still young, we established the tradition of taking annual family ski vacations, which continues to this day. They were also afforded an opportunity for private lessons in areas of individual interest, and both were accepted into Atlanta's finest private schools. Then, in their early teens, something cataclysmic happened: their dad, the quintessential entrepreneur, developed an exciting and expensive new dream that was so compelling that their mom phased out a successful psychotherapy practice to partner with him on a full-time, unpaid basis. And the secure life that they had come to know and trust began to take some sharp dips and turns.

Bill's vision was to take all that we had learned about organizational change, visionary leadership, and adult learning, and develop a delivery system using satellite technology to reach American businesses with what they needed to become global, world-class competitors. The Corporate Satellite Television Network, Inc., (CSTN) represented an innovative, economical way for corporations to con-sistently receive the information and skills they needed to implement Total Quality Management and become a Learning Organization. Through CSTN, companies committed to a vision of organizational excellence would have the ability to implement and execute their plan with a consistent, continuous improvement process.

Delivered nationally by a customized curriculum via satellite tele-vision, sessions would be designed for all levels of management and every employee on a work team. They would be taught by experts in organizational excellence, all part of a "faculty" of master teachers and leading-edge thinkers.

"When the idea first began percolating in my head," Bill related to Merrill Oster in his book, *Visionary Leadership*, "I didn't sleep for days. I wrote, did research, and introduced myself to entirely new communities of people. I also knew I could try to fund this in one of two ways. One way was to continue my existing business and use it to support the new project. But I realized that the existing business would demand too much energy because of the level of commitment every current or future client required. I knew I would be on a tread-mill with my energy in two places. So I fulfilled my current commit-ments and set out with my new vision."

Bill designed a model for the CSTN programming according to how adults learn—one idea at a time—followed by discussion and skill implementation. After assembling the finest business faculty available, we would put their materials into a video format. This *Programming for World-Class Performance* would be available to subscribing businesses eight hours a day, five days a week. Every employee in each organiza-tion would have the opportunity to be trained (as part of a natural work-unit team) on a consistent, one-hour-a-week basis.

Our comprehensive business plan called for a $10,000,000 start-up fund, with an almost equal amount required in phase two. In the quest for venture capital, Bill spent several months lining up three different sources of outside funding. Each of the financial groups wanted a 70 percent share of CSTN for their investment. In one instance, the funding turned into "loans" to be paid back, even though the investor retained controlling ownership. These factors, coupled with the cost of time, attorney fees, and the stress and delays connected with continuing to seek investment capital, led to the final decision to proceed with our own resources and creativity. Although none of us knew the specifics of what might be required, we all knew, up front, that getting CSTN off the ground would require some sacrifice on all our parts.

The Surrendering Process

Although each member of our family knew that some sacrifices would be required in the process, we didn't know that it would require everything we had (including college education funds) and then some! On a gradual basis, as we surrendered every aspect of our financial security in order to get the company off the ground, I was able to see how comfortable we had become in our acceptance of materialism. Then another interesting thing happened: I discovered that, in the process of surrender, I was also losing my emotional attachment to material things. I remember wandering through one of my favorite stores, Neiman Marcus, feeling totally detached from everything I saw, whereas previously I had desired practically every-thing I saw! The dream had become the real and valued thing in my life as well as in the life of almost everyone it touched.

"A compelling vision," relates Larry Dennis, a CSTN affiliate and author of *Empowering Leadership*, "has an urgency that attracts like a magnet. . . . It creates a blueprint of the future and serves as the propelling force of creative change."

And so it was with the concept for CSTN. Almost everyone who caught the vision wanted to participate in some way. Within the first two years, we amassed a group of nearly 30 internationally-renowned experts in organizational excellence, translating their teachings into video-based team-training modules. In addition, an affiliate network of almost 40 well-respected training and consulting organizations was developed to represent the CSTN "Learning Organization" process to their clients. The concept was so innovative and far-reaching that we hired artist Jim Channon to make a rendering of the CSTN vision and structure so that it was actually "seeable." This enabled everyone involved to keep it in focus and to be able to share it fully with others. As Bill learned how to draw the dream, he discovered that making his own renderings was as critical to having it stay vital and real for him as putting it into words.

Through those years, as long as our family focused on the big picture, we were able to stay committed and lovingly do whatever it took to support the dream. This required the ability to maintain a clear vision of the big picture, even when our dream was producing nothing tangible. Consequently, although they were often frightened or feeling ambivalent about the future, our children never lost sight of the values behind the vision.

By the end of her sophomore year in high school, for instance, Vail, like many of her friends, was driving a sporty little BMW and attending an outstanding college-prep institution, The Westminster Schools. When we could no longer afford the tuition for her junior year, Vail was suddenly thrust into the Atlanta Public School System, ranked one of the academically weakest in the entire nation. The physical environment (no air conditioning; filthy rest rooms; cracked walls; windows, and ceilings; insects and pests; etc.) was a form of culture shock. Compounded by the lack of challenge and the get-by attitude of the majority of students and teachers, Vail became bored and despondent, and by the middle of her senior year, our honors student attended only the minimum number of classes required by the state for graduation.

She also suffered the loss of her car when it was totaled in an accident. Since the car had been used as collateral on a loan that went into the CSTN business, it was now the property of the bank. The insurance money that would have replaced it went directly to the bank. Undaunted, Vail decided to get an after-school job and save toward a new car. She was hired as the youngest sales associate at Macy's Lenox Square and quickly became her department's top producer. As it turned out, that job was a Godsend.

Early one morning, I found myself entering my daughter's bedroom with a heavy heart and a painful request. Shaking her gently, I asked, "Honey, can you wake up for a minute?" She rolled over sleepily and opened her eyes. On the verge of tears, I managed to say, "Daddy and I need your help."

"What's wrong?" she asked, sitting up in bed.

"We need $1,000 of your money—today—in order to keep the office phones turned on."

Without hesitation she replied, "Sure, Mom. Go ahead and take it."

Vail's prompt, selfless response pushed my fragile emotions over the top, and I collapsed, sobbing, into her arms. As she soothed and comforted me, we experienced one of several role reversals where she was required to become the nurturing adult, and I became the comforted child.

When Kord was 11, he became a committed tennis player. He began training with a personal coach at the Ansley Golf Club, where we were members, and became their new junior champion his first year. When the club membership and lessons were no longer available to him, he continued in tournament play, armed with little but natural talent, courage, and determination. There was something about his carefree, inspired manner of play that even strangers loved to watch. As Kord competed against opponents whose parents were still making major investments in the latest equipment, drills, and private lessons, we were amazed how he endured this handicap without bitterness and with very little complaint. I will never forget the day, however, after a particularly crucial loss to a highly coached and highly ranked player, that Kord sarcastically voiced his only gripe: "Why don't you go to McDonald's and get a *real* job—with *real* pay!"

The summer Kord was at that precarious age of 13 was one of his toughest times. The two of us would drive back and forth to the State and Southern Championships with almost no money for a place to stay when we got there. One time, we were reduced to sleeping in a dingy room with cracked walls, one small, lumpy bed, and a poorly functioning bathroom. Our one surviving credit card was a gasoline card from Amoco. This meant that fuel for our diesel-burning Mercedes could be purchased only at specific Amoco stations. We had some very tense moments wondering if we would make it to the next Amoco with diesel fuel for 99 cents a gallon. We were also required to obtain almost everything we ate or drank from Amoco food marts. This was rather embarrassing and tedious for a boy who just wanted to be able to do things like the other kids. Even now, years later, we will look at each other, shake our heads, and smile when we drive past an Amoco food mart!

Only you, of course, know your own children well enough to determine when something has significantly changed their readiness level for certain information. The most important thing to communicate is that whatever is going on, this is not about them—they didn't do anything wrong. I am convinced that fully disclosing our situation (the good, the bad, and the ugly!) to our children, and purposely including them in the many decisions which affected their lives, has made them emotionally strong and prevented them from feeling like victims. In the process, they discovered that a person could stay focused on their dreams independent of their circumstances. They learned the life skill that foregoing short-term gratification will eventually result in long-term gain. The end result has been an ability to focus on their own big pictures and attain their own personal goals.

Establishing Your Values

I am also convinced that it was a strong sense of values that helped to steady and guide our family through the severest storms. These family values included:

- Belief in a personal God who knew us, loved us, and cared for us
- Desire to seek and know His purpose in our individual lives
- An attitude of gratitude for the abundance of life
- Loving support of each other in fulfilling our purpose and pursuing our dreams
- Having open lines of communication
- Taking care of our health and emotional well-being

- Making a contribution to the lives of others

I realize that in the midst of the unrelenting challenges of life, it is hard to find the time or words to disclose, even to those closest to us, the values we cherish and the purpose behind the choices we make. This, however, is essential. Our values are the foundation on which a sound home or organization is built. If each of your family or organizational members does not have a crystal-clear picture of the values and overriding dream operating in your household or organization and where they fit into the big picture, stop everything. Make sure that they understand the purpose behind what they are going through. There may be days when that knowledge is the only thing that can propel any of you from your beds!

Values Worksheet

Take the time to sit down together and map out the big picture:
- What do you stand for as a family/organization? What are your values?
- What is the compelling idea behind your business or the way that you earn your living?
- Where are you now? In one month, where will you be?
- What can you expect a year from now? In five years?
- What will it take for you to get there?
- Who will be served by your product or service? How?
- What difference will it make in the world?
- What is the price to be paid? For how long?
- Is it worth it? What is in it for you personally?
- What is in it for your children? (Make sure they know this!)
- How can they share in making it real?
- How can you best serve them?
- What is your individual dream in the context of the big dream?
- What are your individual dreams, independent of the big dream?

Capture those dreams, embrace them, and make them fully yours. When things get rough, you may only be able to serve your personal dream, and not the person or idea behind the larger dream.

Pinpointing Your Mission

Writing a mission statement captures the reason the organization exists in as simple a form as possible. As emphasized by Stephen Covey during a CSTN "Quality Imperative" teleconference, "A mission statement is the beginning of personal and organizational leadership. By referring to it, and internalizing its meaning, we are more likely to choose behavior that serves our values, and reject behavior that opposes them. This creates a context that gives meaning, direction, and coherence to everything else." Although the form of your mission may evolve and change, the underlying vision, if clearly focused, will remain the same.

At the core of all successful mission statements is the ideal of contribution and customer service. Our friend and CSTN faculty member, Gary Heil, co-author of *Leadership and the Customer Revolution,* loves to tell the legendary stories of Stew Leonard, Sr. As the owner of "the world's largest dairy store" in Norwalk, Connecticut, Stew carved their policy on a 6,000 pound rock right at the entrance to the store.

Rule 1. The customer is always right.

Rule 2. If the customer is ever wrong, reread Rule 1.

According to Mr. Leonard, "It's chiseled in stone because it's never going to change." He believes that policy is responsible for the store's growth from a 1,000-square-foot "mom and pop store" into a 100,000 square foot "shoppers festival" with annual sales approaching $100 million.

My favorite mission statement belongs to Federal Express, a winner of the Malcolm Baldrige National Quality Award. It contains four words: "The World on Time." All FedEx employees know they only have one job: to get it there absolutely, positively on time. As a result, I know companies that send mail via Federal Express to the next floor in their own building because they know it will get there when promised and be considered a priority when it arrives!

It doesn't matter a bit whether your "organization" is a business or a family; the principles of vision and the necessity of a mission statement remain the same. Having a common vision of what you value enables you to handle anything the world throws your way. The main hurdle is developing the discipline for transforming each individual's personal vision into a vision shared by all. Dr. Marjorie Blanchard, the dynamic president of Blanchard Training and Development, calls a change goal "a dream with a deadline." A good starting point for any change is:

- Where are we now?
- Where do we want to be at some specific date in the future?

When you forget what it was all about (and chances are you will), your mission statement will serve to remind you why you started this whole venture in the first place. So here are some guidelines to enable you to develop your own organizational and family mission statements.

Mission Statement Guidelines

Remember that developing a mission statement is a dynamic process, involving all those who must make it happen. It is a discovery of your highest self, your values, and your aspirations. It enables each person to "learn how to learn" and motivates him or her to excel—both because they want to and because they are a part of something bigger than they are.

So gather around the conference table or the kitchen table and focus on who, what, and where you are now versus the ideal you envision you can have or be. Develop together a concept of the place that each person wishes to give his or her best to. State clearly what you feel is worthy not just of your time but of your very best for the rest of your life. Weave the words together that express what brings the inspiration, commitment, and loyalty to all that come in contact

41

with your company or family. Paint a picture of the vision you each will enthusiastically contribute to and help make happen. Then work to narrow it down into one sentence or a short paragraph that can be internalized and easily memorized. The following "game" inspired by Merrill Oster, author of *Vision-Driven Leadership*, can help.

Mission Statement Worksheet

1. Have each person write down the five to seven aspects that best capture the essence of your business or family. These should include your economic well-being, love and acceptance values, desire for balance and quality of life, plus challenge and growth opportunities.

2. Compare each individual's statements. Where are the statements similar? Where do they overlap? Do any of them actually say the same thing in different ways, though striving for the same goals?

3. Try combining two or three overlapping statements into a short composite version.

4. Now add another.

5. Continue until you have one very strong statement that encompasses the totality of your group mission.

6. Give it a final test: Does this statement inspire me? (If not, give it some extra punch!) If so, put it in permanent form.

7. Commit it to memory.

This statement now becomes the benchmark by which you determine all future actions and decisions. The only way to convert your values, vision, and mission into action is to "Just do it." Step out from the dream, knowing that it is being sourced by the personal passion you have for your mission. You must believe unswervingly that the world will be a better place when your vision is realized. And this belief must come from within.

Having the Why to Live

When we know the *why* of life, we can tolerate almost any *how*. Out of your values will come the why of what you do, providing a focus for the contribution (the how) of each person. When these values are based on simple, timeless truths, they inspire the best in everyone, even small children. That's why it's vital that values be shared by all concerned. They then become the standard by which life choices and decisions are made.

In difficult times, our tendency is to pull in, adopt a protective mode, and isolate ourselves. Yet when people look out for their own best interests and develop separate points of view, blockage and separation occur. By sticking together and making small day-to-day commitments, however, each member is able to stay focused and take some personal ownership of the dream. Thus a common viewpoint is established, allowing you to see your progress along the way. This creates alignment and reinforces the vision.

I remember years ago being inspired by a beautiful poster of a small sailboat surrounded on all sides by rocks and boulders except for a narrow passageway where the sun was peeking through. The caption read, *The only way out is through.*

Although our tendency may be to shield those we love from the harsher aspects of life, I do not believe this is a luxury we can afford. There are many unknowns in life. For most of us, hardship comes from ambiguity—the lack of context and clarity of meaning. Reality, whatever it is, is easier to deal with than uncertainty. It is essential that everyone stay focused on why they are doing whatever is required of them along the way. With the *why* firmly in mind, each member, in his or her own way, can "bear with almost any *how.*"

Those of you who let your passionate vision and highest values guide you will be empowered to accomplish seemingly impossible things. You convert your vision into action when you act. Step forward from the dream, firm in the belief deep within you that both you and the world will be a better place when your vision is realized. It is then that unseen resources will begin to materialize. This is both a compelling and humbling experience.

Chapter 2

Determining Your Personal Purpose

What is success? I think it is a mixture of having a flair for the thing you are doing, but knowing that is not enough; you have got to have hard work and a certain sense of purpose.

—Margaret Thatcher,
First woman in European history
to be elected Prime Minister

This is the true joy in life, the being used for a purpose recognized by yourself as a mighty one; the being a force of nature instead of a feverish, selfish little clod of ailments and grievances complaining that the world will not devote itself to making you happy. I am of the opinion that my life belongs to the whole community, and as long as I live it is my privilege to do for it whatever I can. I want to be thoroughly used up when I die, for the harder I work the more I live. I rejoice in life for its own sake. Life is no brief candle to me. It is a sort of splendid torch which I have got hold of for the moment, and I want to make it burn as brightly as possible before handing it on to future generations.

—George Bernard Shaw,
1925 winner, the Nobel Prize for literature

THE ABILITY TO DEFINE AND LIVE a purposeful existence is uniquely human. As Dr. Martin Luther King has stated, "Man is man because he is free to operate within the framework of his destiny. He is free to deliberate, to make decisions, and to choose between alternatives."

Knowing and seeking to fulfill your unique life's purpose provides clarity, guidance, and satisfaction regardless of the circumstances. Anytime your focus is on the fulfillment of an ultimate desire, discouragement or depression will seldom overcome you. So take a moment right now to clearly envision your own definition of satisfaction or success in life. What do you really want to accomplish? What pursuit is worthy of the time of your life? What do you see yourself joyfully doing? How do you see yourself doing it?

Vision is not the same as purpose. Purpose is your reason for being. Vision is a picture of a certain future. Purpose is abstract; vision is concrete. Purpose is becoming the best I can be by serving in a particular way.

For instance, the purpose of NASA in the 1960's might have been to advance the exploration of outer space in order for the United States to be the leader going into the 21st century. Vision would be seeing yourself on the moon by the end of the decade. Purpose must have a dream or vision to serve. It is out of your vision that your purpose will arise. They are inseparable.

Knowing your purpose (reason for being) gives instant meaning and direction to your life. It establishes your individual self as part of a larger picture. It builds resiliency to setbacks. Viewed from the context of your purpose, everything that happens to you appears meaningful, rather than as an isolated event. This eliminates failure and despair by transforming "setbacks" into the structural tension that propels the next action.

Distinguishing between Purpose and Goals

Before giving you the guidelines for discovering (or updating) your own purpose statement, I want to clarify the difference between having a purpose and having a goal.

Because we, as human beings, are capable of manifesting design or purpose, we are teleological by nature. We have an innate ability to seek out targets. Setting goals allows us to orient ourselves and operate in relation to a target. Together, purpose and goals form our guidance system, providing an inner picture (vision) of how things are supposed to be.

A goal, by definition, implies some struggle or effort, i.e., "an object or end one strives to attain." Its root connotes a boundary: "to hinder or impede." It's more of a "get to" phenomenon—the seeking of something outside yourself, over there, just beyond reach. Without purpose as the framework, goals imply that where you are is not enough, causing you to constantly seek more. They are often driven by unhappiness, a perceived state of deficit, or fear of failure. With a clear-cut purpose, however, goals become the crucial interim steps by which all progress can be measured. They let you know how you are doing along the way, and give you a basis for keeping score.

Purpose, on the other hand, is a "come from" phenomenon. Once clarified, it is the place you come from in all that you do. It is defined as "the object for which something exists." It is also the object for which you exist, in other words, your reason for being. Each of us has been given unique abilities to make specific contributions here on earth. Living purposefully enables you to continuously do what you love to do. For every unique gift or talent that seeks expression in the world, be assured that there is a matching need begging to be filled.

Your Purpose Is Your Lifeline

The first time I really understood the incredible power of purpose and individual determination of will was when I was reading *Man's Search for Meaning* by Viktor Frankl. To survive the horrors of imprisonment in the Nazi concentration camps, Frankl resolved to use the experience as a "living laboratory" to study human will and its relationship to suffering. He discovered that even in the worst of circumstances, the one thing that couldn't be stripped away was an individual's dignity and choice of action. The right to direct their own energy and determine for themselves some purpose and meaning within the confines of even those unthinkable circumstances was undeniable.

47

"We who lived in concentration camps can remember the men who walked through the huts comforting others, giving away their last piece of bread. They may have been few in number, but they offer sufficient proof that everything can be taken from a man but one thing: the last of the human freedoms—to choose one's own way."

Those with a defined purpose for their life—a book to write, a newborn grandchild yet to see, a mission to fulfill, even revenge toward their oppressors—survived day after day, sustaining themselves through their own faith, effort, and will. Despite the fact that all prisoners were subject to the same inhumane conditions, Frankl observed that "some [prisoners] behaved like angels and others like swine." It was easy to tell, he related, when someone had lost their will to live: they would begin trading their daily sustenance, their meager food, for the momentary deadly pleasure of a cigarette.

If you have not yet read Frankl's remarkable book, I urge you to do so. The time may come when you find yourself thrown into a reversal of circumstance or fortune, such as he was. In such an instance, your purpose will become your lifeline. It will give you the power to manage your fear and remain focused on the big picture.

The Loss of Self

In your heart you know who you are. Yet somewhere along the way, many of us lose sight of our heartfelt purpose for living. And we find ourselves wondering—what happened? What happened to the zest for the dream? What happened to the excitement? When did I stop believing?

A look back at your earliest ambitions can be shockingly significant in revealing the degree and kind of purposefulness you possessed during childhood. These early ambitions are significant because they reflect a time when your dreams were still fresh, noble, and untainted by the disillusionment of life. They reveal your loftiest ideas about yourself, and your deepest longing for meaning.

Take a moment to reflect back on your most vivid and heartfelt childhood ambitions:

- What did you dream of being or doing when you grew up?
- What difference did you want to make in the world?
- What has happened to that sense of purpose?
- How, and to what degree, has it changed?
- How does your childhood dream compare with what you are now doing?

For many of us, the answers to these questions are cause enough to weep. We are all intrinsically aware of our destiny when we are young. We know in our hearts who we are. Yet we know neither why nor how we got so boxed in or off-track through the years. Others of us think we are content in our work, but sense something is still missing. We have forgotten that our essence is giving and our identity is spiritual in nature. We have lost (and are unsure how to regain) our true and highest self.

Some Purposeful Questions

The following questions will help return you to that true, idealistic, and optimistic self, and provide clues to your unique talents and the form of contribution that you are intended to make:

- If your world were perfect right now, what would it look like? What would it feel like?
- If you had all the time and money in the world, what would you be doing?
- What produces ultimate satisfaction for you?
- When, where, and why have you experienced a state of bliss or supreme joy?
- When time flies by, what is going on? What are you doing?
- What activity produces a state of timelessness, a moment of eternity for you?

Reconnect with those times; feel their richness and realness. Focus on the steps you can take to increase this state of being in your daily life. Then ask yourself,

- Do I know what I am trying to do with my life?
- Am I clear what my unique talents and abilities are?
- Do I have a passion for my current occupation or work?
- Would I do the same thing, even if I were not being paid for my services?
- Does my daily occupation lead to a specific contribution to those around me?

Wouldn't it be great to get out of bed every morning answering these questions with an enthusiastic "Yes!" Most people cannot. By following the guidelines below, however, you can discover what brings joy and satisfaction into your life and develop a meaningful purpose statement that will keep you grounded under all circumstances. It is a fun and enlightening process.

Purpose Worksheet

Completing the process below will
1. Pinpoint your natural strengths
2. Determine how you best express these qualities with others
3. Define the contribution you are designed to make

If you don't have a purpose statement, take the time right now to create one.

Guidelines for Determining Your Life's Purpose

List five of your unique personal qualities, such as honesty and enthusiasm. (If an uninhibited child or your best friend were to describe you, what would they say? "I like you because you are so . . . (funny), (kind), (spontaneous), (visionary), (decisive)", etc.")

List two or three ways you enjoy expressing these qualities when interacting with others, such as: supporting, demonstrating, providing, encouraging others or inspiring those around me, etc.

If you were to express those qualities in a perfect world, what would be the result? In other words, what is the result or effect of your unique talents on others? What is the contribution that you would make?

Now combine the three categories into a single statement. For example: "My purpose is to use my (1) visionary leadership, enthusiasm and love of discipline to (2) encourage and inspire others (3) so that my family and employees can thrive in an atmosphere that produces harmony, prosperity, and excellence."

My first purpose statement went something like this:

> *"My purpose is to use my intuition and clarity of vision to support everyone I meet in discovering how magnificent they are and the Source of that magnificence, so that we each experience a life of authenticity, joy, contribution, and love."*

I carried it with me everywhere I went. Anytime I was foggy about who I was or what I was about, I would look at it. Through the years, it has been honed and refined, and I've "upped the ante" a bit since then, but it has always provided direction and guidance for my life. In those moments when nothing seems to be working right or making any sense, it provides a place to return to and remember both who I am and my function in this life.

During tough times, we have difficulty living in the present. We spend a great deal of time dwelling on the past or projecting into the future.

Detecting the Loss of Purpose

Earlier, I referred to your life purpose as your *Lifeline*. That's how essential purpose is to your success in meeting the challenges of life.

I can still remember those times when my highest priority was to make it through another day. Anytime you lose purpose, the following detrimental attitudes may arise:

- **Indecision.** Without vision and purpose to guide you, you will find it very difficult to evaluate courses of action and make strategic decisions.
- **Fear of failure.** The weaker your current purpose and vision for the future, the more fearful you will be of failure. You will not be able to translate present failure into precise, purposeful direction for achieving future goals.
- **Unclear priorities.** Without clarity of purpose, you will find it difficult to have proper or clear priorities. When multiple demands clamor for your time and attention, you must have a way to quickly determine what your involvement should be.
- **Instability.** A lack of purpose causes insecurity, instability, and perplexity when confronted with the greatest challenges of life—ambiguity and constant change.
- **Fatigue.** A lack of energy is a sure sign that you are off-purpose.
- **Self-concern.** Since you can get for yourself only what you give to others, grab that purpose statement and get back on track. You will be the recipient!

The Purpose of Purpose

The purpose in knowing your purpose is that it reveals the source of power, joy, and satisfaction in your life. It gets you back on track when you've lost your focus on the big picture. It serves as a grounding device, both personally and organizationally, by reminding you of your true nature and the contribution you are here to make.

I am convinced that purposeful living is the key to a triumphal and a joyful experience of life, no matter what the circumstances. Purposeful living enables us to embrace, rather than resist, change and the unknown. It becomes not only the foundation from which you live your life, but it guarantees that you can keep your head when, in the words of Rudyard Kipling, "All about you are losing theirs and blaming it on you." It becomes your competitive edge.

Purpose in Action

I once had an amazing life-saving experience of the value of being grounded in one's purpose. I was seated beside my husband, Bill, as he drove up the steep incline of the driveway to our home. He parked the car and got out to come around and assist me. As I was reaching back to take our infant daughter, Vail, from her car seat, the car started rolling down the driveway! I was completely helpless to do anything. Suddenly, Bill opened the car door, and half running, half jumping, got enough into the driver's seat to steer the car away from the brick walls lining both sides of our driveway, and stop the car before we reached the street or the neighbor's house directly below.

In a class he was conducting that evening, which happened to be about purpose, Bill said, "The choice was either to get behind the car and push or to get in and steer. The car represented either an obstacle, or a vehicle, depending on my context and purpose at the moment." And since his purpose was to provide for his wife and his daughter, his response was to steer the vehicle to safety. "Until thought is linked with purpose," wrote James Allen, "there is no intelligent accomplishment."

Let a Barrier Become a Bridge

I have discovered, as I go through life "on purpose," that obstacles along the way are simply indicators of what I have yet to learn. What may look like a barrier can actually become a bridge. Even obstacles can be purposeful when we are living purposely. And when we blend our unique talents with service to others, we experience the ultimate goal: timeless existence and a jubilant spirit.

Chapter 3

Experiencing the Joy of Service

Thou shall be served thyself by every sense of service which thou renderest.

—Elizabeth Barrett Browning

Some people treat life like a slot machine, trying to put in as little as possible, and always hoping to hit the jackpot. But I believe that people are wiser, happier, and have more inner peace when they think of life as a solid, intelligent investment from which they receive in terms of what they put in.

—Roger Hull, Business Executive

> **LIFE PRINCIPLE:**
>
> *The greatest among you is the servant of all.*

THE QUICKEST AND SUREST WAY to break the bonds of discouragement, fear, or grief is to get beyond self-focus by rendering a purposeful service to others. The transforming effect of purposeful service is such that it can be likened to the splitting of the atom and the release of its power or to the discovery of the polio vaccine to free the world from the fear of paralysis. The results are that powerful!

As an entrepreneur, I discovered early on that there are few straight lines or clear job functions in the journey from dream to reality. It is fraught with the unknown. Success often requires everyone to live, breathe, eat, and sleep the dream in order just to survive. Job descriptions become cross-functional, and you learn to wear many hats.

But I also discovered that, in the process, you have the opportunity to ascertain what you are truly capable of achieving. You find yourself becoming what you are committed to producing. And you realize what you are committed to through the results you actually produce.

How Do You View Service?

The word "service" means different things to different people. Whenever I asked my Learning Laboratories students for thoughts or images this word brings to mind, they gave responses such as these:

- being a servant
- being less than or lower than someone else
- performing menial duties
- having someone "lord over you"
- being taken advantage of
- experiencing some form of loss

Do some of these match your own response? Of course. And why wouldn't they? All our lives we have been taught to look out for ourselves, to not let anyone take advantage of us, to take care of "numero uno," etc. If you don't, nobody else will, right?

Well, I hate to think how far this perception has set back the world's ideals for contentment or for human relations. Once these thoughts take hold, they soon form part of our belief system and begin to shape our model of reality—the way we think life is. The belief that "I need to look out for myself" is self-fulfilling: it becomes a reality. In striving to protect yourself, not only can you not serve others, but also they, in turn, can't serve you. People around you begin to protect themselves—simply because you are doing that very thing for yourself. It is a perpetual, self-reinforcing cycle.

Crippled by this perception of service, we spend a great deal of energy protecting ourselves from getting involved with and from truly helping others, even in our most intimate relationships! We become so concerned that we'll be "taken advantage of" that we fail to see the irony in that way of thinking. We spend our time avoiding something that cannot happen. It is possible for someone to take advantage of you *only* if you are looking out strictly for yourself, guarding and protecting what you believe is "yours". In such a situation, you believe that even those who serve you are trying to "use you." When you are looking out for yourself, everyone becomes a threat.

Seeing Service in Its True Context

Breaking free of this perception will require a complete paradigm shift in your thinking. So let's discuss the context of service, because once a shift takes place in how you view "service," your experience of life dramatically changes. When you truly serve, there are no obstacles—because you see everything as serving you in return. Some people seem to have been born knowing this. Not me. I had to go "kicking and screaming into paradise," the paradise of making a contribution beyond anything I imagined possible.

Here's one way the shift occurred in me. At the time we began the pursuit of our new dream of building the global Corporate Satellite Television Network, I was teaching, running groups, and earning $60 an hour as a private psychotherapist. I was happily doing my thing. For me to let this all go and partner with my husband on a full-out, full-time, unpaid basis required a huge shift in my context of service. It required a leap in faith to go from the comfort of a secure, known lifestyle into the abyss of the great unknown. I also had to expand my personal vision of serving others from "individual" to "organizational" and, finally, "global." Making that type of shift is not necessarily comfortable, but it does build character!

So let me ask you: When you began to clarify the focus of your vision and determine your purpose in life, what did you discover? Was your purpose to look out for yourself or to avoid being taken advantage of? Of course not! How foolish it is to serve with the thought or expectation of any quid pro quo. In the end, we can only serve ourselves. Your purpose reflected your desire to make a contribution to others by being taken *full* advantage of.

What if someone did, in fact, take full advantage of you? What would that mean? What do you have for them to take advantage of?

For someone to take full advantage of you implies that there is something within or about you worth taking advantage of, right? Well, of course there is! It's all those gifts, talents, and wonderful qualities that you possess, all those abilities and skills you have worked so hard for all these years that make you worth being taken advantage of, or worth something, period. To whom? Well—yourself, of course. But even more important—to others. To your mate, your children, your friends, your employers, your extended family, your community and church, and the world around you. That's why you're here! That's the object of your existence: to be of service and to make a contribution.

Discovering Your Purposeful Service

Our only true function in life is to serve one another, with love. And when we come from that purpose, the form of our service no longer matters. "You will find, as you look back upon your life," wrote Henry Drummond, "that the moments when you really lived are the moments when you have done things in the spirit of love."

I know women you can't refer to as a "housewife" or a "secretary" and some that don't "do coffee" or "make copies," etc. I even had a housekeeper tell me once that she didn't "do windows." That's kind of like bringing a newborn baby home from the hospital and deciding that you don't "do diapers."

The heart of the context of service is whatever it takes to get the job done. If the job is caring for a home, that includes the windows as well as the toilets. If it's nurturing a baby, it includes late-night feedings and dirty diapers. If it's working in a business, the context of service is the same, no matter what form, role, or hat is required at the moment. Most entrepreneurial businesses require that everyone on board be flexible, creative, and willing to handle more than one task. This poses a problem for those who think, "It's not *my* department (or problem)" or "That's not in *my* job description."

So how do you set aside "self" in order to serve without feeling misused and abused? Unlike the parent who says, "After all I have done for you!" how do you escape the thought that you are making a huge sacrifice? I think it is by first getting beyond the narrow definition of the words *serve, servant,* and *service,* and immersing yourself in their true context. You'll find it in the *Bible:* "He who would be greatest among you is the servant of all." Or in another translation, "Anyone wanting to be a leader among you must first be your servant" (Matthew 20:26).

You know, deep down, that you are the happiest when you are offering the greatest service, when you are a part of and contributing to something bigger than yourself or to someone whose vision is broader than yours. It is just your "ego" that gives you trouble! These words by Richard Alpert (Ram Dass) have pulled me through many moments when I forgot either my true servant nature or my purpose in this world:

When I know who I am, I am you.

When I don't know who I am, I serve one who serves.

In fact, you can only serve one who serves. And in order for one person or group to serve another, they must allow themselves to be served. In other words, they must surrender to being served.

The Relationship between Service and Surrender

The surrender to being served can be a difficult thing for any self-reliant or entrepreneurial personality. In day-to-day practice, it is probably most difficult in male-female (husband-wife, boss-employee) relationships, although it is noticeably lacking within most organizational structures as well. (Just look at the difficulty one department has in serving another within the same company, even though it is their own, direct, internal customer.)

The main source of this difficulty is the notion of the "separate self" so often propagated in our society. I use the word "notion" because that is all it is: a thought or belief that we are separate from each other. This, coupled with the burden and illusion of functions and roles, keeps us feeling and acting separate. Thus we cling to that which separates us rather than to that which creates oneness or unity.

If you stop to examine any well-working relationship, you will realize that the surrender/serve principle is alive and well. I'll illustrate how this principle works by using a couple of examples from my own life.

Encounter with an Entrepreneur

Each of us, I believe, has pivotal events in our lives—turning points—that change us forever. When I first met my husband almost 30 years ago, he was a young man with a mission that did not include having a wife. For my part, I was busy modeling, teaching, and helping to run an agency and studio called the Model House in Kansas City, Missouri. As the offspring of a father who served as a radio minister and a mother who was a talented actress/writer, I had been a performer and student of the dramatic arts since childhood and was, at that time, a speech and theater major at the University of Missouri in Kansas City. I thought I knew exactly where I was heading and what I was going to be, but a "chance encounter" when Bill showed up to give an inspirational talk at one of our staff meetings changed the direction of my entire life.

Bill's first words were, "I don't know any of you personally, but I know some very personal things about you. Each of you desires to be listened to, and you want to feel understood." He then talked about the enormous potential of people, about inspired, team-based organizations, and what it took to constantly go beyond your past best performance. He said that everyone wanted to be a part of a cause that was greater than themselves—and this thought touched something deep within me. I was mesmerized. He was the most committed, dynamic speaker I had ever heard, and I knew even then that I wanted to be a part of his life. At the end of his talk, Bill circulated a sheet of paper and asked us to indicate whether we wanted to attend the impressive one-day Sales and Motivational Congress he was promoting. I wrote a heartfelt "*Yes!*" Two days later, he showed up at my office and asked me to lunch. He said he was "moved by my spirit" and could feel my energy. (How's that for an original line?)

That lunch was one of the most intimate experiences of my life. The minute we were seated at 100 West, a cozy restaurant in the heart of the Plaza, he took my hand and kissed it. Looking me straight in the eyes, he said, "Tell me the most wonderful thing about you." And without hesitation I answered, "My resiliency, my ability to bounce back." (Little did I know how much I would need that quality the next 25 years of our relationship.) We talked for hours. I discovered that Bill grew up in Casper, Wyoming, and had been financially on his own since the death of his father on his fourteenth birthday. Suddenly, he had a mother with no insurance, four sisters, and several uncles who told him at the funeral that he was now "the man of the family." So he began his entrepreneurial life.

Bill and his mother, Marie, began washing dishes in the high school's cafeteria. (Marie is a whole other story. One of 18 children, she was forced to quit school after the eighth grade in order to help out. Although she had no business background or experience, she worked her way up to become the Director of Cafeterias for the Natrona County school system, planning all menus, figuring payroll, and managing a staff of 25. By the time she retired, Marie was overseeing the preparation of lunches for five city schools and distributing meals via specialized vans to six satellite county schools. Although she was given no specific budget, her goal was "to always make ends meet." None of her school cafeterias ever went into the red.) Meanwhile, Bill also started a janitorial service, which is still in business, cleaning buildings and restaurants until 2 or 3 a.m. He lettered in three varsity sports and worked two or three other jobs on the side. Upon graduation from high school, he was honored with both the Worthiest Student and the top academic scholarships to Casper Community College. Amazingly, he also managed to save the incredible sum of $10,000.

I quickly realized that this was an enormously driven and accomplished 25-year-old. As we talked, Bill shared his dream of bringing about lasting change in the quality of life for people in organizations.

He saw everyone he met as helping to serve that dream. For years he had been developing personal mentors, the leading thinkers in their fields, and was able to quickly absorb and implement their ideas.

While at the University of Denver, he recruited, trained, and managed over 100 college students for his direct import company. In his senior year, he co-opened regional offices for a national sales training organization in the cities of Denver, Dallas, and Atlanta. He took several graduate courses toward an MBA and completed the requirements for both a Bachelor of Science and a Bachelor of Arts degree. Upon graduation, he cofounded the National Association of Sales Education (NASE). That's what he was doing in Kansas City—he was in the middle of a 20-city tour of NASE's Sales and Motivational Congress and would be moving on within the next two weeks.

As Bill drove me back to the Model House, I teased him that a young man with an American Express card and a silver-blue Jaguar XKE must have something going for him! In truth, I was already in love. This was the man I wanted to be the father of my children.

A few days later, as Bill's guest, I attended the NASE Motivational Congress. He introduced me to the day's presenters, which included spellbinding Zig Ziglar, the well-known author and speaker. When I met Larry Wilson, the founder of Wilson Learning Corporation and Pecos River Learning Centers, I had the feeling that I was the most important person he had ever met. He had that kind of charisma. Dr. Kenneth McFarland, the winner of the American Freedom Foundation Award, was compelling in his relentless desire to help people reach their fullest capacity. I also heard first-hand the "Voice of America," Paul Harvey. These people were not only big thinkers, they were totally committed to their dream of communicating with and inspiring others.

It was quite a day! Meeting them was like stepping into a whole new world, the world beyond a focus on "self." And I came away with a new personal dream—I wanted to be a part of that world and to contribute on that level.

In retrospect, I realize that by hearing Bill speak and then having him share with me his dream of serving others, I intuitively (and consciously) surrendered to serving his dream and being a part of his life in some form. Then out of my commitment to his dream, Bill naturally began to surrender to and serve our love. One way he did this was by transferring his Army National Guard weekends to Kansas City. Thus the relationship deepened in spite of distance and lengthy periods apart. Please note that in order for me to successfully serve him or his dream, Bill had to surrender to being served. That, in and of itself, was a major accomplishment for his independent/loner entrepreneurial personality.

Here's how it worked in my parents' life. While a young college student, my father and some of his friends saw my (future) mother walk across the campus of Los Angeles City College. "Well, boys," he said, "my future just passed." That was his moment of surrender. My mother's took a little longer, but they served each other faithfully for over 50 years in the give-and-take of marriage. My father's final act of surrendered service was to devotedly care for my mother in their home throughout her terminal illness with cancer. When you are surrendered, the natural response is to serve one another with love.

In Western societies, we grow up with the concept of distinct, separate aspects or functions of what's considered feminine and masculine. We receive many mixed and confusing messages: Men are the strong ones, the providers, the doers. Women are the weaker sex, the nurturers, the receivers. Men are expected to be tough, invulnerable, and capable of handling things by themselves. It is considered feminine to be sensitive, vulnerable, or supportive.

In far-Eastern philosophy, however, "female" and "male" simply represent the negative and positive dualism within all things. Known as Yin and Yang, they represent the oscillating duality of nature. Together, Yin and Yang signify the dynamic interaction that creates all of reality. They are dual expressions of the same principle. In my experience, and in the experience of thousands of the students that have passed through our programs, the context and joy of service are best expressed through this more integrated understanding.

Although traditional wisdom states, "It is more blessed to give than to receive," in truth, giving and receiving are inseparable. You can receive only what you have given. *To give is to receive.* That is where the thought of sacrifice ends and the experience of joy begins.

Discover What Is Needed and Wanted

In order for you to serve your organization, clients, spouse, or your family members, you must allow yourself to be taken full advantage of, no holds barred. You must also find a place where you can serve through your own form of expression. This is best done by looking closely to see what's needed and wanted, and then simply doing it—according to your own personal purpose.

Personal Service Worksheet

1. Restate your personal purpose. This is the framework for all that you do.
2. According to my purpose, there are various needs around me that I can help fill.
- There are needs I see in my organization that I am willing to serve.
- There are needs I see for my clients that I am willing to serve.
- There are needs I see in my spouse or significant other that I am willing to serve.
- There are needs I see in my family members that I am willing to serve.
- There are needs I see in my neighborhood, church, or community that I am willing to serve.
- There are needs I see in the world at large that I am willing to serve.

A word of caution. It is not enough to serve someone else's dream without having one of your own. There are a couple of reasons for this.

1) It is not possible for you to be personally responsible for anyone else's happiness. Each person is the creator of his own reality and is thus responsible for his own dreams and happiness. So make sure

to have your own dream within the context of your spouse/partner's dream or the organizational dream.

2) Forms change. The form of your service or organization may change, although the vision remains the same. If you get caught up in the form of someone else's dream, you are in danger of feeling bitter, defeated, or devalued over something you can't control.

This happened to me after I dissolved my psychotherapy practice to partner with my husband on a full-time basis and establish the Corporate Satellite Television Network. Out of the desire to make our dream real, I jumped in with both feet. It became an all-consuming passion. As vice-president and co-founder, I worked 10- to 12-hour days and many weekends, literally holding the company together when Bill was out of town. When the form that I had committed myself to serving changed from full-time satellite-delivered programming to in-house consulting and implementation of our extensive video library, I was completely lost. I didn't know who we were as an organization, and thus, who I was anymore. It took me well over a year to recover from that sense of loss and to develop my own dream again.

For Bill, the form of what he did was not important as long as it served his vision and purpose. I got stuck in the form of CSTN instead of the contribution it was designed to make to others. The ability to go beyond the form of something—whether it's an image you have of yourself or the kind of work you do—is in itself transforming. It is a source of freedom that allows you to truly serve others.

Source versus Resource

In any committed relationship or business partnership, there is often a fine line separating various job functions. We hear terms like "the power behind the throne" or "the woman behind the man." These sayings describe different, chosen functions and are not value assessments. Usually one performs the function of "source of" and the other "resource to" each other and the big picture. As you source another person's power, you also source your own.

Listen to the definition of each:

- **Source**—that from which something comes into existence, develops, or derives; any person, place, or thing by which something is supplied.
- **Resource**—something that can be drawn upon for aid or to take care of a need.

Do you see how closely they are aligned? They are simply different sides of the same coin, much like "surrender and serve": one objective with two interchangeable functions.

Be an Enabler

I have long known that my main function in this life is to enable those lives I touch to fulfill their personal purpose. So I was startled when my friend Linda jumped to my defense when Bill referred to me as an "enabler." She, perhaps, was responding to the negative connotation of enabler—the enabler who contributes to someone who is living a dysfunctional or destructive lifestyle. So it has occurred to me that if Linda was offended by that appellation for me, I need to establish its broader context, or you might resist it as well.

Here's what *Webster's New World Dictionary* has to say: *enable* 1: to make able; provide with means, opportunity, power, or authority (to do something); 2: to make possible or effective.

Not a bad job description! The sage Will Rogers once said, "We can't all be heroes, because somebody has to sit on the curb and clap as they go by." And it aptly describes me every Fourth of July in Atlanta for the last twenty-some years. I am the one with goose bumps and tears in my eyes, standing at the top of Heartbreak Hill handing out ice and cheering for my husband, children, friends, and another 50,000 runners during Atlanta's annual Peachtree Road Race. It takes only one grateful "Bless you!" to remind me that this simple gesture of support is considered a valuable service.

"There are two ways of spreading light:" writes Edith Wharton, "to be the candle or the mirror that reflects it." Please remember that serving as an enabler or resource to another person is a very high call-

66

ing. After all, who sources the source? You do. *You* are the place the source itself springs from, is fed from, nourished from, and replenished from. Therefore, you, too, are source.

Bake Someone Brownies

You know the story of Helen Keller and how her beloved teacher, Annie Sullivan, enabled her to go from an animal-like child to the inspirational champion of millions of handicapped people. But do you know the story of the other "miracle worker"—the person who was responsible for the healing and humanizing of Annie Sullivan?

Years ago Dr. Otis Maxfield, a Jungian psychoanalyst, told a group of our students this unforgettable story. He said that during his internship, he conducted some group therapy sessions at the Massachusetts State Infirmary in Tewksbury. The hospital was a home for the indigent and those considered hopeless, and many of the doctors saw little of worth or value in their patients. One of the men in his group was a "big, hulking slob of a human being" who had deep psychological illnesses. During Otis' rounds on the ward one day, the man picked up a book and threw it at him. "I wanted to deck him!" Otis related. "I wanted to hit back."

Much to his surprise, an old woman, a floor maid who had been with the hospital since the late 1880's, stepped out from the wall. She walked up to this man and embraced him. Quietly she said, "It doesn't help to throw a book at someone who is trying to help you."

Otis remarked, "I have never seen a more Christian act in my entire life. Slowly, this seething mass of humanity settled down, and the crisis passed."

As Otis came to know this woman, he saw something within her that is not often found even in professional people. One day, she began to tell him the story of Annie and showed him the subterranean dungeon where Annie had been kept. The door was made of iron bars.

"She came here blind and psychotic, more animal than human. I used to bring her trays of food. Before I could turn my back, they were thrown against the wall. She was slowly rotting away because she wouldn't eat. I tried everything to get her to eat something. Nothing worked. She even slashed her wrists with the broken glass.

"One day I baked her some brownies, and she liked them. Because I found something she liked to eat, I was able to start talking with her. After a while, she worked her way out of that dungeon cell and up to some of the higher floors."

Then Otis Maxfield pieced together the rest of the story: After Annie had moved upstairs, some official investigators toured the institute. As the group passed by her bed, Annie strained her eyes to make something out of the shadowy figures in front of her. When they began to move out of sight, she screamed to get their attention: "I want to go to school!" she cried.

"Poor thing," a voice said, and the gray figures faded away.

A few days later, there was a stir in the women's ward. Annie was told to get her things—she was going to go to school. That afternoon, Annie was sent to Boston to attend the Perkins Institute for the Blind. The summer after her graduation, the school officials received a phone call from a man who said he had a daughter who was more of a vegetable than a human being. He was searching for someone to care for her. He wondered if they knew anyone who could possibly learn to love a blind, deaf, and mute child. So Annie Sullivan, "the miracle worker," was sent to the home of Helen Keller.

Many years later, an interviewer asked Helen Keller to what she attributed her lifetime of amazing success. She quickly responded, "To Annie Sullivan, who taught me to love other people."

Then the writer asked Annie Sullivan, "To whom do you owe your success?"

"To an old floor maid in Tewksbury, Massachusetts, who used to bake me brownies, and taught me the power of love."

The Servant Leader

In his book, *Servant Leadership, A Journey into the Nature of Legitimate Power and Greatness*, Robert K. Greenleaf credits his concept of the servant as leader as having come from reading Hermann

Hesse's *Journey to the East*. In this story, a servant named Leo, who does both their menial chores and inspires them with his song and spirit, accompanies a band of men on a mythical journey. Surprisingly, when Leo disappears, chaos ensues. Unable to progress without him, the group disbands.

Years later, the narrator (one of the party) is taken into the Order that originally sponsored the journey and finds that Leo, whom he thought of as a servant, was in reality the untitled head of the Order, its guiding spirit, and a great leader who had simply created his own opportunity to serve

"To me," states Greenleaf, "this story clearly says that the great leader is seen as servant first, and that simple fact is the key to his greatness. Leo was actually the leader all of the time, but he was servant first because that was what he was, deep down inside. Leadership was bestowed upon a man who was by nature a servant. It was something given, or assumed, that could be taken away. His servant nature was the real man, not bestowed, not assumed, and not to be taken away. He was servant first."

Transforming Stopping Points into Starting Places

Quite often, when people join an organization, their single greatest concern is their title. Yet people who are primarily concerned with position can function only to protect and defend their turf. This causes a significant shift away from the purpose of the organization. Such people squander their personal power and create divisiveness and negative energy around them. Personal power comes from the servant nature within one's self, not the bars on the uniform or the title on the business card. These, in fact, can develop barriers to peoples' abilities to learn and serve. It is when we forget ourselves that we can do something everyone else will remember.

The concept of the leader as servant is so essential, to both personal and leadership development and to the success of organizations, that we designed it into the curriculum of the MBA degree in Organizational Leadership which our company, Learning

Laboratories, established with Brenau University in Atlanta. One course, entitled "Human Resource Management," was devoted to servant-as-leader principles. The course work included a weekend-workshop practicum that focused on mastering the context of service in everyday life by successfully serving other students.

What we discovered from this course of study was that, for each of us, there is a point beyond which we think we cannot go, or will not go, in the service of others. Yet for these students, what was initially their stopping place soon became their starting point, simply indicating a limit-to-growth they had each placed upon themselves. In the process of the course, they learned what it means not only to expand their educational horizons but also to truly extend themselves.

Out of these experiences there arose a personal validation of the words of one of the most influential men of our lifetime, Dr. Albert Schweitzer, world-renowned humanitarian and winner of the 1952 Nobel Peace Prize:

"I don't know what your destiny will be, but one thing I know: the only ones among you who will be really happy are those who will have sought and found how to serve."

Chapter 4

Committing to Commitment

The moment one definitely commits oneself, then Providence moves too. All sorts of things occur to help one that would never otherwise have occurred. A whole stream of events issue from the decision, raising in one's favor all manner of unforeseen incidents and meetings and material assistance which no man could have dreamed would come his way.

—William Hutchinson Murray,
Leader, Scottish Himalayan Expedition
to conquer Mount Everest, 1951

> **LIFE PRINCIPLE:**
>
> *When you step out in faith, through commitment and deliberate intent, the universe works in concert to support you.*

EMBRACING THE UNCERTAINTIES OF LIFE is similar to climbing Mt. Everest: it is not possible to "accidentally" achieve either of these feats. You can do them only when you have an unswerving commitment to a great purpose.

Now that you have a context for service and can articulate your life purpose in a concise, inspiring statement, you have a solid foundation for staying tenaciously focused outside yourself and on the big picture. You know your reason for being on this earth, and what you are capable of producing. You have clarified your vision for the future and articulated the values you wish to live by. This is where the dynamic principle of commitment comes in.

Commitment breeds tenacity in the face of failure and the ability to see setbacks as merely temporary. When we act from deliberate intent, a dynamic inner change occurs. By making up our minds about something, we truly set the universe, or Providence, in motion. Complex, subtle forces beyond our ability to comprehend become engaged in the process. As we move forward and demonstrate enthusiastic determination in the pursuit of our dreams, we allow the "force that wants us to realize our destiny" to kick in. We apply the *principle of favorability*.

I love the simple way this principle was explained by Melchizedek, the old King of Salem, to the shepherd boy, Santiago, in Paulo Coelho's magical story, The Alchemist:

". . . there is one great truth on this planet: whoever you are, or whatever it is that you do, when you really want something, it's because that desire originated in the soul of the universe. It's your mission on earth."

"Even when all you want to do is travel? Or marry the daughter of a textile merchant?"

"Yes, or even search for treasure. The soul of the world is nourished by people's happiness. And also by unhappiness, envy, jealousy. To realize one's destiny is a person's only real obligation. All things are one. And, when you want something, all the universe conspires in helping you to achieve it."

"That's the way it always is," said the old man. "It's called the principle of favorability. When you play cards the first time, you are almost sure to win. Beginners luck."

"Why is that?"

"Because there is a force that wants you to realize your destiny; it whets your appetite with a taste of success."

The principle of conscious commitment keeps vision and purpose consistent in our day-to-day lives. I cannot tell you the number of times commitment alone has kept me (and sometimes my marriage) going. I am convinced that fidelity, commitment, and loyalty are some of the vital lessons I was personally meant to master in this life. During the long and very difficult period when our financial resources

72

were depleted and our home was being threatened with foreclosure, although my husband, Bill, would constantly remind me that he loved me dearly, I could neither hear nor feel it. I simply felt numb. When the pressure of sustaining our organization without adequate funding and the weight of being responsible for the livelihood of our staff and their families was most intense, Bill would project his stress onto me, becoming extremely difficult to live with. The only thing that pulled either of us through these and other instances was the fact that, years ago, in a garden wedding ceremony, we had said, "I do"—and then we kept choosing to do what we had committed ourselves to doing.

If I had to boil down the secret of successful long-term relationships it would be this: keep choosing each other every day. We have all been given an amazingly potent gift—the power of choice. It's our God-given birthright. The important thing, no matter what, is to keep choosing. Choose each other through the sameness, the madness, the devastation, the sorrow, the joy. And when you choose someone or something, choose it with all your heart. Don't be faint-hearted. There is no power in half-hearted, unenthusiastic choice. Embrace it all—that's what the commitment "for better or worse" means. That's why it is a staple of traditional wedding vows. It's based on the realities of life. When you give your pledge, you give your word. It then becomes the basis for your thoughts and actions.

The context of commitment is whatever it takes. By definition, it is a combination of "to bind as by a promise" and "to put to some purpose." As the act of giving and keeping your word, commitment is the very heart of integrity. In concept alone, this is a very powerful thing. In practice, it is an essential principle for leading a happy, productive, and fulfilled life. Commitment sustains relationships, transcends time and matter, and is the very essence of being able to love, give, and accomplish.

In the *Bible*, John begins his *New Testament* account by affirming God's creative activity. Do you remember his first statement? "In the beginning was the word." The *Genesis* account reports that "God said . . . and there was. . . ." These are very telling, revealing statements because, likewise, in the beginning, there is only your word: What you say you will do, according to your purpose. This is at the very heart of personal integrity, as well as the beginning of the creative process.

Reflection Worksheet

There are two words that are so powerful that we can manifest in life whatever follows them. Think about this for a moment. Think about what that means. Then think of all the ways you use these two words to form a descriptive phrase about you, about those around you, and about your status in life. The two most powerfully creative words in the human language are—*I am.*

What declarative statements do you make that determine your behavior? your destiny? your well being? How do you describe yourself to others? How do you declare yourself to yourself? What do you normally find yourself saying?

For example do you say: "I am so tired, angry, depressed, discouraged, beat, sick, bored, upset, worried, stumped, broke, frustrated, etc. What words do you actually use?

What effect do these words have in your life? What effect do they have on your spouse, children, co-workers, employees, clients, suppliers? What about the effect on your finances, weight, success, decisions?

When you are with your children, what do you say in reaction to the things that they do? For instance, when they do not do their homework, practice the piano, or behave respectfully, do you find yourself saying, "I am sick and tired of your behavior."

What happens next? Possibly threats. You become a policeman and must carry out a punishment.

As a result, they see themselves as no good, a failure, or a problem, and become more rebellious and difficult to communicate with. You become depressed, lose your energy, wonder "why bother."

When you think of the key people in your life, what do you hear them saying? What descriptive words do they use? What results are they producing?

Never say a thing about yourself or others that you don't want to see realized. We bandy about phrases in our everyday life without a thought for their consequences. We even have a new phrase: everything is "to die for!" Do we really want to "die" for a piece of double-chocolate chocolate cake?

My purpose here is not to imply that our words and thoughts are always negative. It is to point out how frequently we make unconscious statements without realizing or remembering their potential impact. When we state "I am" (anything), we affirm (declare positively) that whatever follows is true. The problem is that our subconscious mind doesn't know that. It doesn't know we are just bandying about some meaningless phrase to describe our attitude or feeling at the moment. Our mind interprets this as reality. And it responds to any vividly imagined message it receives in an effort to make it real.

This mechanism can also be used in a very conscious and positive way. The word *affirm* means "to present as fixed," "to make valid," to "assert to be true." When we consciously and purposely affirm something, we make a positive declaration that it is a current reality in our life. We are, in effect, exercising faith and belief in our inherent potential and our vision for the future. When we commit ourselves to our vision by stating it as a positive current reality and vividly imagining the desired outcome, we firmly imprint the desired change by fixing it in our memory. It is the genuine, passionate intent behind the words that makes the difference.

Out of pure, unyielding intention and fixity of purpose, amazing things are accomplished. A wonderfully moving example is the inspiring story of a young Canadian runner named Terry Fox, which has been made into a movie. Two days after his eighteenth birthday, Terry was told that he had cancer and would lose a leg. Despite the shock and speed with which his life turned upside down, Terry wasted no time in accepting what had happened. He quickly sidestepped the trap and futility of self-pity by shifting his focus from his limitations to his possibilities. Out of this crisis, he determined a new reason to live and a purpose so strong he was able to accomplish an extraordinary feat.

Wearing an artificial limb, Terry ran over 3,300 miles across Canada—the equivalent of a marathon a day—until he could run no more. His desire to raise one million dollars for cancer research through a Marathon of Hope initially inspired contributions of over $30 million. Today it lives on in the lives of tens of thousands of Canadians who run annually to raise money for cancer in his behalf.

Terry said, "I guess that one of the most important things I've learned is that nothing is ever completely bad. Even cancer. It's made me a better person. It's given me courage and a sense of purpose I never had before. But you don't have to do like I did—wait until you lose a leg or get some awful disease, before you take the time to find out what kind of stuff you're really made of. You can start now. Anybody can."

What is equally remarkable, we are told, is that Terry considered himself to be an average person. Although he set a magnificent example for us all to follow, he sincerely believed he was basically an ordinary person. What Terry exemplified above all was the emotional muscle of courage. He had the heart to rise above his outer circumstances and self-limitations to do what he felt must be done. And in the process, he experienced the deep satisfaction and joy of going beyond anything he had thought possible.

When I speak about commitment, I don't mean just being committed to some "thing," such as a person or a dream, which might change or not be what you perceived it to be. What is required is commitment to commitment. This is the spirit of authentic, deliberate intent that creates a dynamic change inside you. That's what turns an intention into a reality. Intention implies "having something in mind as a plan or design." Reality refers to "the quality or fact of being real." They are not one and the same. There is often a huge gap between something we intend to do ("Well, I was going to . . . gee, I meant to . . .") and the actual accomplishment of it.

Throughout life, we are either producing reasons or results. The reasons are our excuses, our "why nots": why we didn't, couldn't, etc., do what we said we would. This keeps us in a constant state of victimization, ineffectiveness, and blame. Results, in the final analysis, are the only real evidence of our true intentions, and in our society, results determine success. That's why success is a numbers game; keeping score tells us how we're doing.

I have referred to the entrepreneurial life as one of uncertainty, and that, of course, is true. But it is even more accurate to say that *all* life is uncertain. At one level, that's all there really is, no matter who you are or what you do. These are the givens, the things we can count on: uncertainty, constant change, high levels of risk. The state of uncertainty is seldom comfortable. The mind craves certainty. It wants to know outcomes. It functions to protect us by pushing us to take the easy way out. As a result, the opportunity for a quick fix or the temptation to follow the path of least resistance will always present itself as an attractive option.

Any time you step out to accomplish something, you will find conflict, potential obstacles, and illusions of resistance. All that we can count on, really, are the principles we live by. They are the only variables that are relentlessly stable, fixed, and unyielding. We can choose to be fearful and withdrawn, or to be focused on learning, growing, and contributing to the world.

Some people hesitate to commit themselves out of the fear that they will lose something they don't even have. This can be true on the level of relationship or with any other aspect of life. If, for instance, the fear of losing your freedom or independence causes you to avoid commitment to a relationship, you are already living in bondage and are, in fact, not free. Even the phrase "risk to win" is a misnomer. There is no risk in losing something you won't have until you receive or win it in the first place!

Freedom and Responsibility

Only by being responsible are we free. We cannot be responsible, however, for someone else. I learned long ago, from Dr. G. Hugh Russell, that we can be responsible only *to* others, and *for* ourselves, not the other way around. What a relief that was—especially as a parent! For instance, as a parent, I am responsible to my children to provide an environment of love, support, moral example, and whatever information and guidance they require to make wise choices in their lives. After furnishing and modeling these behaviors, I am not responsible for their choice of action or behavior. I am, however, totally responsible for my own thoughts, actions, and behavior.

This context was particularly helpful during a period in his teens when my son, Kord, insisted on having long and droopy (so I thought) hair. As his parent, it was my responsibility to him to point out that people—rightly or wrongly—judge us by appearances, and that it could be to his disadvantage to look sloppy or unkempt (he thought casual and cool) in several real life circumstances. For instance, should he be stopped for a traffic violation, his appearance could cause a police officer to go harder on him than if he presented himself as a totally clean-cut kid. Although he chose to ignore my advice at the time, I was not responsible for whatever consequences that choice might have brought to him.

All choices, of course, have consequences. Several months into the development of CSTN, we were running short of personal investment funds and had not yet secured venture capital. My husband and I decided to take out a jumbo mortgage on our almost-paid-for family home of 13 years. A lot of love had been expressed and traditions developed in our home over that period of time. Yet, at the closing, when faced with the possibility that at some point we might not be able to make the payments, it did not seem like an insurmountable risk. We were both able to say, "It's just a house." Our context was that those cherished memories were within us, not within the walls of this particular address.

Discover New Paradigms

During this same period we discovered that, once the dream is there, everything that goes on in our lives serves it in one way or another. Even our inability to make a mortgage payment served the dream by forcing us to discover a whole new set of resources. We had to discover new paradigms. We had to go to a whole new level and ask ourselves once again, "Are we still committed to the dream? Is it worth risking our house and causing our family to live in grave uncertainty?" To succeed, you must find a whole new way to look at things. You must create a new set of relationships from all of your old relationships. You make the dream real by speaking your word with authority and taking action. Each step generates the next one.

Commitment gives us new power, no matter what may come to us—disaster, sickness, or poverty. The enormous power generated by applying the principle of deliberate intent is best expressed in this cogent commentary by W.H. Murray:

> Until one is committed there is hesitancy, the chance to draw back, always ineffectiveness. Concerning all acts of initiative (and creation), there is one elementary truth, the ignorance of which kills countless ideas and splendid plans: that the moment one definitely commits oneself, then Providence moves too.
>
> All sorts of things occur to help one that would never otherwise have occurred. A whole stream of events issues from the decision, raising in one's favor all manner of unforeseen incidents and meetings and material assistance, which no man could have dreamt would have come his way.

I have learned a deep respect for one of Goethe's couplets: "Whatever you can do, or dream you can, begin it. Boldness has genius, power and magic in it."

Being Equally Yoked

Another aspect of purposeful commitment is reflected in the Biblical principle of selecting partners with whom you are equally connected or "yoked" in your mission, vision, and values (see 2 Corinthians 6:14). This ancient wisdom applies to both intimate relationships and business partnerships and, when subscribed to up-front, can save you a great deal of pain and anguish downstream. I have found, in both organizational consulting and premarital or marriage counseling, that this is one of the first things that needs to be addressed.

An organization that has effectively mastered and utilized this principle of commitment is Alcoholics Anonymous. It is an essential ingredient to AA's amazing and enduring success. After AA members commit to sobriety, they are required to break all ties with the past by telling their old friends, their drinking buddies, good-bye. They can no longer stay yoked or bonded in old, symbiotic relationships of mutual destruction because they are no longer committed to the same things.

What Do You Want—and Why?

To illustrate how often simple commitment and the power of our word is at work in our everyday lives, I have often posed the following problematical situation to my students: "I am holding two ice cream cones in my hands. One is chocolate, and one is vanilla. Which one do you want—and why?"

Going around the room, each class participant responds by choosing one over the other, giving me their reasons for doing so. They have included such things as, "I just like it better," "Chocolate is definitely better!", "It tastes better," or "I just always have."

When pressed further as to why they preferred one over the other, they would inevitably respond, "Well, just because I do!" And that, in fact, is the only reason: just because—just because you made it up and said so.

I trust these principles because I have lived them and reaped the benefits many, many times. "Because I said so!" is not merely something you tell your kids when they've got you stumped, and you don't know what else to say. It's what will get you through those days when you are frightened, full of self-doubt, or unsure what the dream was all about. It is also an experience of the power of your word, the basis for integrity and alignment, and the beginning of the creative process. I'll tell you more as we go along.

For now, I'll leave you with a story of the chicken and the pig who were having a conversation about commitment: The chicken said, "I'm committed to giving eggs every morning." The pig said, "Giving eggs isn't commitment, that's participation—giving ham is commitment!"

Chapter 5

Seeing Everything as a Resource

Gratitude unlocks the fullness of life. It turns what we have into enough, and more. It turns denial into acceptance, chaos into order, confusion to clarity. It can turn a meal into a feast, a house into a home, a stranger into a friend. Gratitude makes sense of our past, brings peace for today, and creates a vision for tomorrow.

> **LIFE PRINCIPLE:**
>
> *Everything you require is already available for your use.*

—Melody Beattie, *Gratitude: Affirming the Good Things in Life*

When you step into absolute uncertainty, through faith—You open yourself to limitless resources.

—William J. Schwarz, as quoted in *Vision-Driven Leadership* by Merrill Oster

ONCE YOU HAVE A PURPOSE TO SERVE, you can begin to see how everything around you is serving that purpose. This is a marvelous frame of reference for life! When you define what's important to you—your values, your vision, and your purpose—and commit yourself to their passionate pursuit, then information and resources you may have blocked out or considered nonessential can take on new significance. Like the shepherd boy in *The Alchemist*, you can activate the force that wants you to fulfill your destiny, setting into motion the law of favorability and the law of cause and effect. Let's look at how these unfailing principles can work for you and propel you toward the achievement of your heart's desires.

Everything Serves Your Dream

The thing that will put you on the leading edge is the context of seeing everything in your life—no matter how you currently judge it—as serving your dream. When you see that everything around you is there to serve you, obstacles miraculously become assets and resources. There is a contextual truth that nothing around you is a threat to you, and everything exists to serve you. Coming from this understanding, you will experience some amazing things. When you allow yourself to respond creatively and intuitively to opportunities, one opportunity will naturally lead to another, and every time a door closes, you will discover resources that you couldn't see before. It's not that they weren't there—you just couldn't see them.

A Case in Point

In December 1987, eight months after incorporating the Corporate Satellite Television Network, the opportunity arose to make our international debut at a large conference and exposition in New York called Training '87. The idea was to take our management/marketing team and video production crew to New York and tape live interviews with each of the featured authors, keynote speakers, trainers, or consultants of note. This would attract audiences to our booth and introduce all the conference participants to the concept of CSTN. It would also provide us with video footage and invaluable relationships with potential CSTN faculty members and affiliates. The whole thing, however, had to be pulled together in two weeks time.

As everyone worked together in spirited, creative action, potential obstacles were overcome, and all the details were handled. This entailed securing three connecting exhibition spaces and furnishing them from scratch. Banners were created, backdrops designed, portable display satellite dishes were built and their transport arranged. All other furnishings (carpeting, plants, chairs, platforms, etc.) were determined and ordered. Meanwhile, dozens of phone calls were made to the offices of keynote speakers and training dignitaries all over the country, with appointments for interviews being set at 30-minute intervals.

Then came the first stumbling block. Due to the strict control enjoyed by New York's electrical union, the installation and working of all lights, camera, monitors, and other equipment necessary for the shoot would have to be personally overseen by a member of that union (charging top union prices and almost doubling our costs). When we pulled everyone together to brainstorm a solution for this devastating situation, our engineer, Walt Snead, had the inspired idea of joining the New York Brotherhood of Electrical Workers! He did, and then he served as the overseer of our entire project.

When all the hotels near the convention center were either sold out or exorbitantly expensive, our producer, the late Patrick Mars, contacted the Waverly Hotel in his former neighborhood, Greenwich Village. Since it was in need of and undergoing renovation, he was able to book everyone into it on short notice—and at a very modest price.

The conference went amazingly well, with almost all of our objectives being met. One highlight was when a distinguished-looking Englishman came to the booth, making inquiries into the nature of CSTN and its purpose in the training world. So Bill and I spent several days getting to know Peter Ross, an executive with the Rank-Xerox Corporation in England. Peter became so intrigued with the idea of a joint venture between the two organizations that he arranged for Bill to come to England to explore the possibilities. This thinking impacts the growth and financial future of our organizations.

Assessing Your Resources

All levels of living require resources. I remember an acting role I played in college—Cinderella's Fairy Godmother. Talk about using whatever was at hand! A pumpkin for a coach, mice for footmen, an old tattered dress transformed into a beautiful gown for a ball. In the blink of an eye and with the wave of her wand, she transformed Cinderella's dull and impoverished world into a magic fairy tale. And so can you, by starting wherever you are, with whatever resources are on hand.

Resource is an extraordinary, spiritually contextual word. Its root, "source," comes from a Latin verb that connotes "rising or lifting up." The prefix "re" means "again." The word has come to mean "a source of supply for enabling something to be carried on." Resources enable you to move forward and accomplish your task.

Anytime you experience a setback and are feeling deprived or stuck, a resource reality-check can get you unstuck. It is here that we begin applying the *law of least effort* (the principle of doing less but accomplishing more) by accepting the premise that this moment and these circumstances are exactly the way they should be.

When my husband was still a young man, it became his heart's desire to start a company committed to meaningful organizational change. The aspect about the National Association of Sales Education (NASE) that disturbed him was that, no matter how powerful the insights or ideas, a one- or two-day motivational congress couldn't bring about lasting change. The inspiration and ideas didn't last because there was no implementation process in place to back them up once the participant returned to the workplace. Bill had come to realize that transformation comes from within, from personal inner change, not from outer stimulation. He envisioned a "learning laboratory" where executives could gain high-leverage leadership and management skills from nationally recognized experts on a consistent, once-a-month basis. These live presentations would include extensive question and answer sessions regarding the actual implementation of the concepts, and in-depth, programmed learning materials would further reinforce them.

Although his funds were completely tied up while dissolving the NASE partnership, Bill took a $250 cash advance from his VISA card and another $250 from his MasterCard to incorporate Learning Laboratories. He stayed where he was at the time (Birmingham,

Alabama), contacted the people he knew, and got started. His greatest assets were a creative mind, personal credibility, and huge determination. These, coupled with the strength of his mission and vision—to "help others learn a better living" by developing a University of Continuing Education—provided the momentum to get started.

Bill's commitment and willingness to move ahead with whatever resources were at hand prompted me to also leave NASE (I had by then left the Model House and was heading up the NASE Indianapolis program) to join him and open Learning Laboratories offices in both Dallas and Houston, Texas.

Six months later we established our fourth Learning Laboratories office (as newlyweds) in Atlanta, Georgia. Within a year's time, we were able to offer college credit for our popular classes. Participants not only received undergraduate credit for attending the sessions, but their companies paid for it through their tuition-reimbursement program.

The following year, Bill and one of our associates, Daryl R. Conner, were asked to intervene at West Georgia College during a major administrative change within the University System of Georgia. They did such an effective job that an unprecedented partnership evolved between Learning Laboratories, a private corporation, and the University System of Georgia. Soon we were able to offer our corporate clients an entire Master of Arts degree program in Psychology and Organizational Development. And all of a sudden, Learning Laboratories was, indeed, a fully accredited "University of Continuing Education."

It was the commitment to keep stepping out with the resources at hand that allowed us the opportunity to discover and validate the principles and practices contained in this book. As Bill and I responded to the real-life personal and organizational challenges presented by thousands of clients and students, we began to see these laws and concepts work—almost mystically—in their lives.

You've probably heard Mary Engelbreit's prudent counsel to "Bloom where you're planted." Well, that's exactly what two Atlanta housewives decided they would do. Marge Fowler and Judy Jones took all their givens: homes and families to care for, a love and appreciation for art, two talented artists in their car pool, a mailing list of 1,500 names—and made those givens work for them. Once a year they do a major art show, turning their homes into galleries for a very popular and profitable event. They are now in their eighth or ninth year, and they exhibit the work of over 30 artists.

The late Steven Hill, another Atlanta entrepreneur, started Independent Commercial Environmentalists with $5,000 he borrowed from his mother. He promptly spent it on bi-fold, eight-color business cards and brochures. Outrageous? Perhaps. But for Steve, this was essential. Those marketing materials were the stabilizing factor that gave him a sense of identity, a place to come from that represented who he was and the quality of service he provided. This, in turn, allowed him to go out each day and knock on doors, quickly building the confidence of his clients and creating a million-dollar business.

Although I don't have a magic wand, you yourself have two priceless resources at hand that can do as much as a Fairy Godmother to turn seeming setbacks into stepping stones. One type of resource comes from the gifts and current "givens" of your life; the other comes from the riches of your Rolodex. Both fly in the face of convention by defying the limiting thought "I can't do this" or its opposite, "I've got to make it on my own." You can't make it on your own, and you don't have to. You were never meant to. As God (George Burns) said to the honest grocer (John Denver) in the movie *Oh, God*, "That's why I gave you each other."

So let's look at the resources you have at hand while we keep the law of least effort in motion. This law is triggered by an attitude of acceptance of your current reality, coupled with an intention to be responsible for it without blaming anyone or anything. Then you can respond creatively to the situation as it is now by discovering and seizing the "precious present" hidden within this moment.

Assesment Worksheet

Begin the assessment by asking yourself: "What are my 'givens'—my current circumstances?" "What is not working or seems lacking in my life?" Write your answers down in specific terms. This begins the process of accepting things as they are at this moment, rather than dwelling on the way you wish they were. Now acknowledge, without placing any blame, your responsibility for being in this situation. You are responsible for it because it is yours. Next, acknowledge within your heart and mind that within every problem there lies the seed of opportunity. What might your great opportunity be?

Ask, "What material resources do I have on hand? What special talents or gifts do I possess? What services could I provide? Who could use what I have to offer?"

What are your human resources? Who do you know (including friends, relatives, and acquaintances)? Who do they know? Whose names and numbers are in your address book? Who is in your circle of influence? Who is in your debt? Where might you collect a favor?

Allow yourself to get outside your accustomed view of reality by taking action on the level at which you are currently living. Many of us stay stuck by waiting for circumstances to change before taking any action.

Expand your vision. Don't be afraid to ask for help. People love to help! Strategic problems call for helping hands.

Your Desire Must Be Bigger Than Your Circumstances

It's not enough to have a good idea—it's the burning desire that triggers commitment, action, and results. The principle at work here is positive expectancy, the law of intention and desire. Pure intention has the power to transform by organizing its own fulfillment. As articulated many years ago by Napoleon Hill, the author of *Think and Grow Rich*, "All achievement must begin with an intense, burning desire for something specific." That's where vision, purpose, and commitment come in. During your quiet period each morning (you do have one, don't you?), ask yourself, "What is my desire for today? How do I intend to accomplish it?" This will serve to heighten your resource awareness and help you stay wide open to a whole range of possibilities.

All action creates cause, and all cause creates effect. This is the law of cause and effect. That's why you must step out in faith and take action. You can't reap what you don't sow. "Positive forethought is a habit of highly successful, causative people," author and consultant Lou Tice reminds us. "They see the outcome as constructive; they reiterate it over and over in their minds, and then they go out and create it."

You don't have to nail down every detail nor have all your ducks in a row in order to step out. Yet don't cling to a rigid idea of how things are going to happen or try to force solutions. If you get rigidly attached to something, you could shut out a whole range of possibilities. Thinking you have the solution to a problem can become an even greater problem in that it thwarts the ability to recognize other resources. When you are dependent on something, it becomes a block to the creative process. So if someone says "No" or something goes sour and looks like a setback, be grateful. Thank that person or circumstance within your heart for having served you. Then step out again into your limitless resources.

Hidden Opportunities

To manage the dream, you must take care not to view the things that are happening as good or bad, but simply as data. Any time you feel a sense of deprivation, simply refocus on—and give thanks for—what's around you. Acknowledge not only the things that seem potentially helpful, but those that look like obstacles, as well. The obstacles could be hidden opportunities.

As entrepreneurs, Bill and I discovered that things that looked like lifelines could actually be more like quicksand. On the other hand, things that looked like negatives or dead ends often turned out to be the lifesavers. My challenge to you is to begin to get outside the "nine dots" of your current circumstances. By operating in a state of intention coupled with uncertainty, you are able to attract and stay alert to unseen opportunities.

None of us ever knows when or where opportunity will surface. One way Bill and I have learned to train ourselves to see beyond the obvious is to play the card game Solitaire with a more dynamic, non-traditional twist: anything already exposed or visible is usable in any combination. In other words, a card that is already on the board in a king or ace sequence can be reentered into the remaining hand if it fits into that sequence and adds another potential option for continuing the game. Playing this way has taught me that I may think I've lost and the game is over, but in reality there are still previously overlooked options available. These are the options that are normally invisible or not available through the traditional and more linear playing rules. They are actually created by giving up gains made earlier in the game on the chance of opening up potential new options. I like it because it adds another element of risk and is a lot like life. And, like real life, we are sometimes required to forgo short-term gratification for the long-term gain.

I know it is not easy to put yourself on the line and embrace the unknown. Those of you who are sailors know that sometimes you have to tack back and forth in order to move forward. On Lake Lanier, where we sail, the winds are quite fickle. We are seldom sailing directly toward our desired destination.

Getting More from Life

Benjamin Franklin once defined as rich "He that rejoices in his portion." I have learned that to get more from life, I must appreciate more of life. It's an ancient spiritual law. I remember how eternally grateful I felt for that one remaining Amoco credit card that provided not only the diesel fuel for our transportation needs but also a way to secure food for my family.

Even if your circumstances are devastating and you feel fragile to the point of breaking, it is imperative for you to be appreciative right now. However ghastly things are and as resistant as you might be to see the other side, force yourself to see through the hurt and haze. You are rich in things all around you. What are they? Stop for a moment and look at the abundant gifts and resources of life that you presently have. They are there serving you, but perhaps you've failed to see them. The moment you acknowledge them—and are grateful for their presence—they (and more) are readily available to you because you can see your life from a higher perspective and are then able to recognize so many more choices. "If the only prayer you say in your life is 'thank you'," Meister Eckhart reminds us, "that would suffice."

An Attitude of Gratitude

During the past year, I have been keeping a Gratitude Journal as an integral part of a daily study using Sarah Ban Breathnach's *Simple Abundance, A Daybook of Comfort and Joy*. I began by selecting a blank journalizing book that depicts the famous painting "Angel with Lute." Although I initially set about my task of acknowledging things I was grateful for by listing five things each day, I now use a less structured format. For instance,

- I'm so grateful that Bill's computer didn't break when Tigger (our cat) pulled it onto the floor this morning. That would have been a disaster.
- Our backyard waterfall garden is as appealing on a cold rainy winter day as it is on a warm sunny one—each day brings its own beauty.
- I did a big grocery shopping today—so different from the days when I had to see what I could do with ten dollars! Although I am still cost conscious, it's lovely to know I can get most anything I want. We had king crab legs for dinner—they were yummy.
- This is Martin Luther King's birthday. I read an editorial written by an Atlanta middle school teacher describing his shock that most of his students didn't really know what MLK did or why they had a holiday today. Then he realized that the kids were experiencing, on a daily basis, the results of King's life and sacrifice. MLK's impact on civil rights has become the norm and their accepted way of life.

- Having a husband who can fix things is a great blessing. Thanks, Mr. Plumber!

The more we notice and acknowledge the things we have, the more we receive. The principle from Chapter 1, "Focusing on Your Vision and Values," comes into play here. The principle works, by the way, whether our focus is "positive" or "negative" in nature. By dwelling on what we don't have, our energy is focused on lack or scarcity, thus generating a greater "lack" by limiting our options, building barriers, or holding us back by our fears. By adopting an "attitude of gratitude," we allow God's grace and abundance to be fully present.

The higher our desired level of living, the more resources we require. What is your desired level of living—not just financially, but spiritually and emotionally? As you determine what constitutes these "higher levels" for you, you begin to connect with the resources that can enable you to live life on those levels. You might want to go back to your original vision or purpose statement, and let it serve as a reminder of the life values that emerged in that process. Resources required for expanded living are not identical with resources for surviving or merely existing in life.

Over 70 years ago, Stuart Chase posed this question: "Are you alive?" He then distinguished the differences between "existing" and "living," and set forth qualities such as creative action, expanded perception (context), and having vital companionship as characteristics of living. He considered himself existing when he was doing things automatically or for self, when he put up with poor communication and misunderstanding, or when he settled for less than his best.

These are tough lessons. When we can see ourselves going in a direction that does not serve others, we are then able to see the correction we need to make in ourselves. The moment we make this shift (through integrity and our purposeful service), then we are living life at its fullest. What we receive is determined by what we have given—times ten! There is nothing to get, only a discovery of what is already there. All we have is all we need. The instant we focus on getting more, we lose our vision and the ability to access resources.

Then, what was an available resource can become a counterforce to the fulfillment of our dreams.

Like Mytle and Tyltyl, the children in Maxwell Anderson's play (based on Maurice Maeterlinck's) *The Blue Bird*, we tend to go out into the world looking for the Blue Bird of Happiness, only to come home discouraged and empty-handed and find that it was in our own back yard all the time.

"Become a possibilitarian," wrote author and minister Dr. Norman Vincent Peale. "No matter how dark things seem to be or actually are, raise your sights and see possibilities—always see them, for they're always there." As you focus on the abundance rather than the lack in your life, an inner shift in your reality will begin to occur. To your awe and amazement, you will find that the miracle you have been seeking has started to unfold.

Practical Life Application

Unlock the fullness of life by beginning your Gratitude Journal. This is not just a good idea: it is an essential tool. It provides a practical reality check, even in the bleakest of times, by acknowledging what is working in your life and opening the way for more. Smile to yourself as you write.

Seek out a special blank book with a cover that has particular meaning for you. Each night before going to bed, write down five things that you can be grateful for that day. How did you progress toward the realization of your dream? Savor the small details. Don't forget the categories of health, home, family, pets, friends, food and shelter—or that you made it through another day. Say it simply and feel it deeply.

Chapter 6

Learning to Let Go

In detachment lies the wisdom of uncertainty . . . in the wisdom of uncertainty lies the freedom from our past, from the known, which is the prison of past conditioning.

—Deepak Chopra, *The Seven Spiritual Laws of Success*

Let go of the place that holds, let go of the place that flinches, let go of the place that fears. Just let the ground support me. . . ."

—Stephanie Kaza, *The Attentive Heart*

> **LIFE PRINCIPLE:**
>
> *To have what you want, you must first release your emotional attachment to it.*

ONCE WE HAVE MADE A WHOLEHEARTED commitment to move toward the fulfillment of our dreams through purposeful action, we must learn to release our emotional attachment to the outcome. Yet learning to let go has been the toughest area for Bill and me to master. Most entrepreneurs have an inherent tendency toward independence, self-reliance, and the desire to feel in control. We trust ourselves, learn to depend upon ourselves, and often create that kind of trust and dependency in the people we attract to our work. It is hard for us to surrender the "delivery details" of our desires. This can create a false security, and even a trap. Like great artists throughout time, we can only receive the full fruits of our endeavors by first releasing our creations to the world.

In order to illustrate the effects of holding onto something, I would like you to stop reading for a moment and do this simple exercise:

Focus for a moment on the most natural process of life—the intake and outflow of your breath. Allow yourself to gently breathe in and gently breathe out. Do this several times. Then, with the next intake of air, consciously hold your breath for as long as you can. As you block the flow of air, notice how desperate you become when shut off from the source of life, and how that connection is resumed only when you are willing to let go of that breath and take in more air

This illustrates what happens when we try to control or hold on to the people or things in our lives. What you hold on to—has a hold on you. The following examples from my own experience demonstrate how unfailingly this process works.

When my husband turned 40, his "midlife crisis" was physical in form but spiritual and emotional in nature. Always a bit of a loner and trusting only himself for his success, the pressure, strain, and weight of constantly generating and maintaining his educational and consulting business—even though he knew he was helping others—began to feel like a heavy burden. His mother, Marie, always said, "Things get worse before they get better"—and she was right. The cumulative effect of this loner stance was blatantly physical. His back became so full of tension and strain that he could hardly stand up. He was giving talks, teaching classes, and working with clients while wearing ice packs on his back. There was little his doctor could do, explaining that the cause was wholly stress-related.

The turning point in this situation took place in Destin, Florida, where we were training a hotel management group and taking a family vacation. Bill had been plagued with excruciating back pain for weeks, and he knew he couldn't continue to function this way. As he and I were walking slowly together on the beach, he turned to me and said, "I feel like I have spent the first 40 years of my life wandering alone in the wilderness. I can't continue to do this any longer."

In the near distance, I saw black storm clouds gathering on the horizon, quickly moving toward us on the deserted shore. In an attempt to beat the downpour, I decided to run to our nearby beach house for shelter. When I reached the porch, I turned around to see Bill collapsed on his knees, completely devoid of strength. A torrent of rain poured down around him.

For an indeterminable amount of time, he remained crumpled in a heap on the sand, appearing humbled by and fully surrendered to that commanding, relentless Force, so much more powerful than he. Then, although it was still raining, the sun broke through the clouds, and a healing stream of sunlight shone directly upon him. When finally he looked up, his face had a shining, unearthly glow. And when he stood, his back was straight and free from pain.

That experience of complete surrender caused an integration and spiritual transformation in Bill. The shift that occurred, he said, was from "feeling driven to do God's work" to forming a spiritual partnership that would "allow God to work through me." And that, as the poet Robert Frost once said, has made all the difference. It was a turning point, not only in Bill's relationship to God but in the way he approached business as well. From this new spiritual partnership came the freedom to expand his Vision, out of which the concept of a new global training organization, the Corporate Satellite Television Network, emerged. It also solidified his personal commitment to serving Life. The burden and struggle were miraculously gone.

Although this experience had a transforming effect in our lives, continuing to let go in other areas was still a difficult thing to do. I have often contemplated why. I think there are several reasons.

For one thing, surrender is more than an "event"—it is an ongoing process. This involves daily, moment-to-moment choices to give up emotional attachments to results, and constantly remembering that you aren't the source of your own power. This goes against the entrepreneurial mentality and may also not seem right or not feel natural to you. Unfortunately, when we forget and begin to rely on our own limited thinking rather than the loving, all-knowing wisdom of God—regardless of our formal religious affiliation or lack thereof—life can look hostile to us or full of scarcity, and so we suffer.

There is also the tendency to develop a vested interest in our projects or dreams. It is not our desires we need to let go of, but our emotional attachment to their outcome or results. The example that follows illustrates the difference between a time when we spontaneously trusted opportunity versus a time when we reverted to a controlling, protective mode.

You will recall from the last chapter that I related how, in only two weeks time, our fledgling organization, CSTN, creatively pulled together and overcame numerous obstacles in order to have a very successful national debut in New York City. You also may recall the English gentleman representing the Rank-Xerox Corporation who became so intrigued with the possibility of a joint venture between our two organizations that he arranged for Bill to come to England to explore the possibilities. This was a marvelous opportunity to become internationally positioned and to gain strong financial backing early in CSTN's development, and we both felt a strong inner prompting that he should go.

However, without realizing it, there had come a point where this new dream that we had been willing to risk our financial security to achieve was no longer just our business—simply a corporate entity. It had become our creation—our "baby." We conceived it, birthed it, nurtured it, grew it, guided it, and even protected it. In that process, we became emotionally attached to it. We forgot that we were merely stewards over it and began to think of it as *ours*.

So when we were approached with the possibility of a joint venture, we were initially grateful for the opportunity to be so well-connected and to have such solid financial backing. As things progressed in England, however, it began to look as if the large conglomerate wanted too much, too big a piece of the business, and too much control. The fear set in that the company would no longer be *ours*. And Bill decided to say "No."

Since attachment stems from a need to cling to the "known," all attachment is either to forms or to symbols that represent "more." This failure—not to trust, not to let go and let partners expand the marketing and production of our training materials—resulted in overwhelming financial pressure that almost caused us to quit. In our willingness to step out again into the unknown—the arena of unlimited possibilities—we were spared from operating out of the dead-ended mindset that "We can't do this because. . . ."

In order to receive the greatest blessings, you have to yield all aspects of your life and your organization as well. The life principle at work here, the law of detachment, was expressed by Jesus through the analogy of a piece of grain. In order to tell his disciples why he must die and leave them, he explained that unless a kernel of wheat falls to the ground and dies, it remains only a single seed. But if it dies, it can produce many seeds. After his death and resurrection, as you will recall from *New Testament* stories, this principle was further demonstrated through the prolific ministry of his disciples.

Each of us has our kernel of wheat—our gift, our dream, our talent, our loved one, our organization. When we forget where this precious kernel came from, we tend to think it is ours alone. It then becomes very tempting to hold it in our hands, to delight in it, to feel it, to know it is ours. The problem is that if we keep it there, that's all we have—one kernel of grain.

In the words of Derek Prince, from his book *The Grace of Yielding*, "You can put your name on it, you can put your label on it, you can go on claiming it as yours, but you'll never get more." The alternative—to drop it, to let it go down into the earth out of sight and out of control—can seem pretty harsh. "Let that little corn of wheat that you hold in your hand fall to the ground and die," he continues, "and God will take care of the consequences."

I find a passage on "Children" from Kahlil Gibran's *The Prophet* equally adaptable to anything we create. Try substituting the word *dreams* for children in the following passage, and see if you agree:

Your children are not your children.
They are the sons and daughters of Life's
longing for itself.
They come through you but not from you,
And though they are with you yet they
belong not to you . . .

You are the bows from which your chil-
dren as living arrows are sent forth.

As with our children, there are times when it is crucial that we let go of our dream—our project, our business, our loved one—and entrust it to the care of others. The ability to release personal attachments to our creations requires us to see them as something outside ourselves, with a life and identity all their own. It is appropriate to relinquish a portion of what may seem like ours for the sake of the whole. The old saying that "All of nothing still equals nothing" is true.

We must allow ourselves to let go. I know this can be a very difficult thing to do.

The Monkey Syndrome

An amazing story is told about the capture of monkeys in Africa. Historically, monkeys presented a major challenge to the foreigners who tried to catch and export them for various business enterprises. Then they discovered a major flaw in the personality of monkeys. Once a monkey had a piece of food in its grasp, it was tenacious in its desire to hold on to it. This inspired the hunters to devise an innovative trap. They placed food into a small cage with bars that a monkey could reach through, and left it in plain view where monkeys were known to frequent. Once a monkey had its hand in the cage, it refused to let go of the food. That's how monkeys came to be their own captors.

The Release of Emotional Attachments

Emotional attachments keep us bound and limited. They predetermine our thoughts, actions, and commitments. Anytime we look outside of ourselves for our identity, we give others total power over our lives. As long as we are concerned about what others think of us, we are owned by them.

The following philosophy and tool provides a proven way for you to release the seven basic areas of emotional attachment: mother, father, family, teams, spouse, self, and children. I learned this release process in the early 1980's from Joyce Hovis. She is a powerful and visionary woman who decided to take charge of her happiness and emotional well-being by discovering a way to free herself from the influence of life's external circumstances. At the time I met Joyce, she was teaching the release process to large groups of people in her Atlanta home. She is now the founder and director of TROB, Inc., a global school of self-knowledge. Not only did I find personal value from use of the release process, but I used it successfully for several years in my private psychotherapy practice. With her gracious permission, I am including the basics here for your use and benefit. For a more in-depth understanding of her work, I highly recommend Joyce's book, *Take Charge and Live*.

The first step is to see clearly your emotional attachments and the control they have over your life. Then you can let each one go. The results of releasing your emotional attachments can be one or all of the following:

- Freedom to make fundamental choices based on what's best for you and what allows you to grow your business
- A greater awareness of current reality
- An increased capacity for decisive leadership and the ability to recruit powerful people into your organization, and ultimately
- The strength that comes from self-knowledge and self-realization

Physically Independent—Emotionally Attached

"Once we begin living our lives apart from our parents," Joyce admonishes, "we believe that we are free to make our own choices. We may be physically independent, but emotionally, this is far from the truth." "Some people avoid dealing directly with the problem by escaping or repressing their feelings," she continues. "They rebel, resist, manipulate, or fantasize. More destructive escapes include insanity, disease, alcohol, drug addiction, and even death. By trying to escape the trap, we only strengthen its control and power over us.

"It is important to recognize that letting go of these attachments does not mean abandoning or betraying our loved ones. It means the removal of control and the beginning of freedom in our relationships. It is letting go of these attachments that takes the struggle, effort, and will out of change. Letting go frees us to be able to make our own choices. We find that we do not have to move in order to get away from interfering in-laws, ex-spouses, or any other unpleasant relationships. We are, in fact, able to love them and be loved by them on a deeper level."

We begin with mother. In my psychotherapy practice, I discovered that people who decide to change often want to start with what *appears* to be their most problematic relationship. What appears to be going on, however, is often not what is *really* going on. An attachment to a mother, for instance, could create problems with a spouse in ways that are not easily understood.

For instance, the first Thanksgiving of our marriage, Bill became miffed at me and could not understand why I was not getting up at four o'clock in the morning to start making our Thanksgiving dinner. I had no idea what he was talking about. My mother certainly did no such thing. But this was a habit of his mother's (thanks to a strong German work ethic and five children to feed) that had become a ritual, which Bill then turned into an expectation and the thought that I was a neglectful wife.

The Seven Attachments

Mother. The first and most influential emotional attachment we have is to our mother, and it is this attachment that controls our thinking. We are with her even before birth, and closer to her than to any other human being for the first few years of our lives. Her thoughts become our thoughts; her opinions, our opinions. Her concepts of us become our concepts of ourselves. Because of our close attachment to her, we know how she thinks without her having to verbalize her thoughts. This gives her enormous power over us.

There comes a time when we either don't have her there to make our decisions for us or want to be free to think for ourselves. We want to be able to turn within to find solutions, to form our own concepts, and to make decisions based on the existing circumstances of our lives. Yet it often consumes us with guilt if we go against her thinking. By releasing our emotional attachment to her, we free ourselves to think the way we choose to think.

The truths and principles our mother taught us will always be there for us as a source of information. Her knowledge and wisdom will forever be recorded in our minds. This can be called upon at will, yet we want to feel free from guilt, blame, or feeling bad whenever we choose to make choices different from hers, or from those she would want us to make. Once the break is made, however, the caterpillar turns into a butterfly and then is free to soar. If the break is never made, the person remains an emotional child in an adult body for the rest of his or her life. Soaring becomes impossible, and blame becomes a way of life.

Father. The second most influential person in our life is our father, or whoever substitutes for him in our lives. It is his responsibility to protect us and teach us how to act in the world. He does this by example and teachings. For our early physical and emotional well-being, it is important that we have a father role model. Our father's actions become our actions. But if this attachment is not released, as adults we are not free to act the way we want to act, nor are we free to do what we want to do. Rebellion is the one exception. If we rebel against him, we will act just the opposite of the way he acts, but we will still not be free to do what we want to do. The decision to rebel and refuse to give your father what he wants prevents you from giving yourself what you want, and everyone else what they want.

Not only do we act like our father, but we want others to act that way, and we become critical and judgmental of their actions. In marriage, for instance, a woman unconsciously wants her husband to act the way her father acted if she is still emotionally attached to him. If he was domineering, she wants her husband to be domineering because it is comfortable and familiar to her. If she marries a gentle, noninterfering, noncontrolling man, she will unconsciously try to make him act like her father. A more extreme example is the daughter of an alcoholic or otherwise abusive father who selects and then stays with a man who demonstrates these characteristics.

Family. The third emotional attachment is to our family. Family includes brothers, sisters, grandparents, aunts, uncles, cousins, etc. Your family dictates how you should, ought to, and have to be. Family influence can be great or small, according to the control they have over us. This control, which began in childhood, is stored in our sub-conscious minds and unknowingly still runs our lives. Family stories about whether we were truly loved and wanted at the time of our birth have an enormous impact on our early feelings of self-worth. Although it was always told jokingly, for instance, my parents delight-ed in telling how, after my arrival on the scene, my older sister tried to hit me over the head with the little mallet from her toy pegboard.

The family is the training ground for learning and perfecting com-petition. Our greatest competition can, and often does, exist within the family itself. Each child competes to be number one with his par-ents. If a sibling feels jealous of or competitive with you, you are auto-matically influenced by his or her not wanting you to be successful or have fun. You may be hard-working and success-oriented, but you may find taking the ball across the goal line very difficult, if not impossible, figuratively speaking. To the world, you may appear successful, yet to yourself, you fall short of achieving what is success for you. This keeps you always striving and never arriving. The joy of success and feeling of excitement that comes with beginning new goals totally eludes you.

Teams. Our fourth emotional attachment is to our teams. Teams consist of friends, co-workers, athletic teams, religious groups, club members, schoolmates, etc. Teams are our entry into the world and teach us what we can have. They mirror us to ourselves by giving back to us what we've expressed to them about who we are and how we want to be treated. If we think highly of ourselves, our teams will, also. If we think poorly of ourselves, our teams will be contemptuous of us.

Because our teams have the power to tell us what we can or can-not have, we are not free to have what we want when we are emo-tionally attached to them. According to our team's rules, we hold back from giving our highest and best, and in so doing, we block our-selves from having everything we want. The fear of being left out, of being different, or of being rejected by the group often causes us to slow down on our road to success.

Natural leaders may refuse to lead, due to the fear of being disliked or excluded. Capable workers may hold back for fear of losing friendships and alliances. Conformity becomes a reality because of our emotional attachment to the group. The fear of being different keeps us from taking risks and having what we want. Those who cannot have team relationships because of childhood programming become loners and deny to themselves their desire to be on a team. They often take pride in their rugged individualism and independence.

Spouse. Our fifth emotional attachment is to our spouse. One symptom of being attached to our spouse is that we are unable to rely on ourselves or, more important, on God. We have a compulsion or need to rely on our spouse and others. Need creates demanding expectations, followed by disappointment, hurt, anger, resentment, and even rage when the expectations are not fulfilled.

Men rely on women for admiration, sex, love, domestic comforts, companionship, and children. Women rely on men for love, financial and emotional support, sex, and companionship. Their priorities are, therefore, different. The reason the marital relationship is the most difficult one in which to achieve success is that it unites two people with different programming on an intimate level. The pressure of living up to preconceived role concepts is enormous for both husband and wife. This can create conflict, blame, the seeking of lost luster outside the marriage, or settling for less than they want.

By letting go of the emotional attachment to your spouse, you can begin to find the solution to what you've always wanted: the warm and loving relationship that was begun and lost. It frees you to rely on yourself for your own identity instead of depending on your partner.

Single people often feel pressure from their family and society to find a spouse by a certain period in their lives. Others need a spouse in order to feel okay about themselves. By releasing the need for a spouse or the need to remain single, the individual will be free to marry for the right reasons, or be free to remain happily single.

Self. Our sixth emotional attachment is to our ego self. The ego self is a false identity that the mind has created. It exists to have its own way and to protect itself at all costs. It is concerned only about its survival. In all its forms, the ego self can keep us from expressing our highest and best self. When we are constantly judging ourselves as to how well we are doing, how we look, and how we are coming across to others, it is impossible to experience the joy of service.

Being attached to the ego self causes inner stress, tension, and anxiety, which often manifest as physical problems. Many turn to pills and alcohol to relieve this, rather than dealing with the cause. By releasing our emotional attachment to our ego self, we take the responsibility to begin freeing ourselves from these enormous restrictions.

Children. In our well-meaning attempt to protect our children from physical and emotional hurt, we often give them our fears and lack of faith. The responsibility for nurturing children and providing for their physical needs is so consuming that it can prevent, or at least inhibit, the normal enjoyments of life. The birth of a child can also interfere with a couple's enjoyment of each other.

Many couples have children for the wrong reasons. A lot of women feel that they should have children because society says it's their duty. Others face an unexpected or unwanted pregnancy. Sometimes parental desires for grandchildren are so great that couples have children in order to please their parents. Feelings of discontentment, resentment, boredom, or even contempt may arise when you have children because you feel you should, ought to, or have to. Releasing our emotional attachment to our children gives us the freedom to enjoy their progress. We can then allow them their mistakes as well as their successes, and we can then allow them the freedom to learn from their mistakes without interference from us. We also then become free to enjoy our children while they are with us, and we are then free from the innate fear of losing them when they are grown.

The Releasing Technique

The releasing technique is a simple sevenfold pattern for releasing your internal programming. It is systematic and orderly. You will be able to observe the natural succession of this pattern. Once you have released your emotional attachment to your mother, the doing and judging patterns of your life will immediately emerge. These patterns also relate to your father. Once you release your emotional attachment to your father, you will immediately stop judging, and you will become aware of being bothered or irritated about how others are being, which relates to your emotional attachment to your family. Your awareness will begin to expand as you release each emotional attachment.

The simplicity and power of this technique is incredible. Thousands of people have used it successfully to remove blocks that were preventing them from creating the kinds of lives they wanted. It has worked for them—it can work for you.

Using Mother as an Example

Using the emotional attachment to mother as an example, take the following three steps:

Step one: Sit in a comfortable position, totally relaxed. Close your eyes, and give yourself the mental or verbal suggestion: "I am completely relaxed. I see myself sitting by a bubbling brook, leaning against a large oak tree. I am so relaxed. I am so peaceful."

Now, put your attention inside yourself to that spot where you go when you think deeply about something or when you pray. See yourself in a scene with your mother. It can be a childhood scene or a recent scene. It can be happy or unhappy. Allow any scene to come into your mind without forcing it. Become involved in that scene. If your mind is blank and refuses to give you a scene, visualize a photograph of your mother.

As you become involved with the scene and re-experience the emotions relating to your mother, you will feel a tension begin to build in your body. It may be in your stomach, chest, throat, or head. If it is in the stomach, chest, or throat, it will rise toward the top of your head to be released. This will happen naturally. All you have to do is visualize it happening and allow it to go.

If your mind begins to resist, ignore it and release the attachment anyway. Say, "Dear Heavenly Father, I totally release my emotional attachment to my mother unto You." If you have a problem calling upon

105

your Heavenly Father, say, "I totally release my emotional attachment to my mother to the universe." Choose the words that work for you.

Imagine that there is a muscle in each temple on the sides of your head. There is actually no muscle there, but it feels as if there is. Relax that imaginary muscle, and release the emotional attachment to your mother into the arms of God or into the universe.

You will actually feel the tension move up and out through the top of your head. It will be accompanied by a feeling ranging anywhere from peace to joy. You will feel lighter and clearer. Colors will be brighter. All bodily tension will go, and you will feel relaxed.

If, after going through the releasing technique, you still have tension anywhere in the body, except the neck or shoulder area, you have not released the attachment. Simply go back inside and do it again. If the tension continues after two or more attempts, ask yourself if you feel that you deserve to be free and happy, or if you feel that you are abandoning or betraying your mother by releasing the emotional attachment to her.

Release any of these blocks by using this technique. Because you have needed your mother's permission for everything, you now have to make up your own mind that you are going to release your emotional attachment to her without her permission. Then you are acting on your own. You are not abandoning her, but you are preparing yourself to have an adult relationship with her versus a mother/child relationship. She will feel the pressure to be the perfect mother for you removed from her, and your releasing your emotional attachment to her will, in fact, help her relationship with you to flow much more freely.

While writing this, I am reminded of an incident that occurred after I first released my emotional attachment to my mother using this technique. My mom, bless her soul, was very good at having expectations and then creating guilt when they were not met. One of the ways she did this was by expecting our family to observe all birthdays and traditional holidays throughout the years. Consequently, as an adult on my own, I found myself experiencing extreme pressure to never forget Mom's birthday, Mother's Day, etc. Rather than gestures of love, these had become rituals of obligation and, should I forget them, guilt.

A couple of weeks after doing the release process, I received a phone call from my mother. While asking me how I was doing, her voice sounded pleasant but perplexed. I responded that I was doing great, and I inquired about her. She responded that she was fine, but that she had been worried about me since this was the first time in almost forty years that I had failed to give her a Mother's Day card or gift! Then I realized that, as a result of the release process, I had felt no obligation to do what I had dutifully done for so many years. I explained about the process and how it allowed me to no longer think of her just as my mother but more as my friend, and she seemed very pleased about that. I assured her that it had nothing to do with my love for her, and that, in fact, I felt even closer to her than I had for a very long time.

Step two: Accept your mother just as she is. Every mother does the best she knows how at that moment, regardless of how it may appear to you or to anyone else. Even if your mother is perfect in your eyes, you will still want to accept her just as she is. Acceptance accomplishes two things: it acknowledges her just as she is, and it frees you of negative thoughts and energies created by your lack of forgiveness. To accept her, go back inside to that spot inside your head, see her clearly, and say, "I totally accept my mother just as she is." Relax the 'muscle' on either side of your forehead, and the acceptance will automatically go into your subconscious mind and flow down into every cell of your body.

Step three: Accept that you are free to think for yourself. Go back inside your head and say, "I totally accept that I am free to think for myself," and allow the acceptance to flow down into every cell of your body.

When you are ready and willing to begin the release process for yourself, the following abbreviated worksheet should provide a helpful guide. Anytime you feel any person or situation "push your buttons" or "pull your strings," you can be assured that this is an indicator that you would greatly benefit from the release process.

Releasing the Seven Attachments and Accepting the Seven Acceptances

Mother

Release: "God (or Heavenly Father or whatever words feel comfortable to you), I totally release my emotional attachment to my mother unto You."

Accept: "I totally accept my mother just as she is." "I totally accept that I am free to think for myself."

Father

Release: "God (or Heavenly Father or whatever words feel comfortable to you), I totally release my emotional attachment to my father unto You."

Accept: "I totally accept my father just as he is." "I totally accept that I am free to do what I want, to act the way I want."

Family

Release: "God (or Heavenly Father or whatever words feel comfortable to you), I totally release my emotional attachment to my family (brother, sister) unto You."

Accept: "I totally accept my family just as it is." "I totally accept that I am free to be the way I want to be. I totally accept that I am free to be me."

Teams

Release: "God (or Heavenly Father or whatever words feel comfortable to you), I totally release my emotional attachment to my teams [be specific] unto You."

Accept: "I totally accept my teams just as they are." "I totally accept that I am free to have what I want."

Spouse

Release: "God (or Heavenly Father or whatever words feel comfortable to you), I totally release my emotional attachment to my spouse unto You."

Accept: "I totally accept my spouse just as he/she is." "I totally accept that I am free to rely on myself." "I totally accept that I am free to rely on God."

If You Are Single

Release: "God, (or Heavenly Father or whatever words feel comfortable to you), I totally release the need or desire for a spouse (or not to have a spouse) unto You."

Accept: "I totally accept that I am free to be married if I choose to."

Self

Release: "God (or Heavenly Father or whatever words feel comfortable to you), I totally release my emotional attachment to myself unto You."

Accept: "I totally accept myself just as I am." "I totally accept that I am free to say what I want." "I totally accept that I am free to express my talents and abilities."

Children

Release: "God (or Heavenly Father or whatever words feel comfortable to you),I totally release my emotional attachment to my children unto You."

Accept: "I totally accept my children just as they are." "I totally accept that I am free to enjoy myself." "I totally accept that I am free to enjoy everything."

If You Don't Have Children

Release: "God (or Heavenly Father or whatever words feel comfortable to you), I fully release unto You the need or desire (not) to have children."

Accept: "I totally accept that I am free to have children if and when I want them."

The Power of Releasing Four Times

Our beliefs begin with a thought. The thought then becomes a feeling. The feeling then becomes a habit, and the habit then becomes a mood. In order to completely release a concept or an old belief, it is important to release it four times: once for the thought, once for the feeling, once for the habit, and lastly, for the mood. It is equally important to accept the corresponding truth four times for the same reasons. For example, if you are releasing the belief that you are ineffective, let it go four times, and accept that you are competent and decisive four times.

Forgive Yourself and Move On

Everyone has individual attachments beyond the basic seven. New attachments can be created at any age. As you have discovered, Bill and I became attached to our corporate creation, the Corporate Satellite Television Network. There is another difficult, even burdensome, area of letting go—I'm referring to our individual conscience that can unrelentingly haunt us for the violation of a moral or ethical principle. I imagine that most of us have done something that either greatly embarrasses us or shames us and that we deeply regret. Our first response is to go into denial. Even if we know we must take responsibility for all our actions and not blame our behavior upon either our childhood conditioning and experiences or upon influences from the external environment, we can have great difficulty in confessing our behavior (where appropriate), seeking forgiveness, accepting the consequences, forgiving ourselves, and letting it go. Since this is the only way to free ourselves from the resulting fear, self-condemnation, or guilt we are experiencing, we must learn to seek forgiveness from God and any we may have harmed and to make restitution for even our most inexcusable behavior. Make it right, where you can, and move on.

Self-forgivness Worksheet

Step 1: Think of the thing in your life that you are most embarrassed about or where you feel the most shame, regret, etc. What effect has it had on your consequent behavior or your peace of mind?

Step 2: Acknowledge how you have been denying or rationalizing the situation. What have been your excuses?

Step 3: How can you now take responsibility for your behavior? What can you do to rectify the situation or to lessen whatever harm your behavior has caused another?

Step 4: What would be the outcome of your doing that? How would things be different?

Step 5: Who do you need to talk to and seek forgiveness? (Yourself, others, God?)

Step 6: What is your commitment about this? What is your action plan? What will you do, and by when?

Step 7: How can you now move on? (Use the release process above; write it all on a piece of paper, and then burn it; affirm daily your wholeness and completeness, etc.)

The truth does set you free. It takes a mature, responsible person to admit, "Yes, I did it, and I am ashamed. I am committed to doing better next time." Remind yourself, "I'm not that person anymore." As Maya Angelou has been quoted as saying, "I did then what I knew then; when I knew better, I did better."

The Surrender of a Burden

The lowest point in my life came at the height of our worst financial period. As the costs to operate CSTN continued to escalate, we took a jumbo mortgage on our home to invest in the company. When the savings and loan company holding the mortgage abruptly folded, all its dealings were taken over by the government-run Resolution Trust Corporation (RTC). Suddenly, we were no longer valued clients but a number. It was impossible for us to meet their threatening demand for full repayment, and there was no room for negotiation. Not only did we receive a notice of foreclosure with a date for the impending sale of our home on the courthouse steps, but I had not yet been able to find a satisfactory place for our family to live. I was also contending with a lump in my breast, complicated by the loss of our insurance. Then one morning I woke up to discover that our cars, which we had offered to the RTC as additional collateral, had been repossessed—they just disappeared in the night.

While I was feeling fragile to the point of breaking, a precious, spiritually grounded woman, Julia Conway, came into my life. Having been apprised of our situation, she could see that I was desperately fighting to keep my head above water. Tenderly taking my hands in hers, she looked me straight in the eyes and said, "Laurie, you are in the midst of a storm of life. The winds are blowing every which way, and your craft is being dangerously tossed about. There is nothing more you can do to figure things out or try to hold them together. The tempest is all around you. Why don't you lie down in the boat for awhile, and rest with Jesus?"

That night I gratefully released my burdens, and for the first time in a long while, slept in heavenly peace. In times of constraint, when we have no direct control over our affairs, we must simply trust, acquiesce, and wait it out.

Some time later, when I read the following words by Jacquelyn Small, I understood the truth of what she was saying: "True positive thinking is the mental stance of surrender, simply trusting the process. We learn to accept what is."

As much as we long to hold onto whatever constitutes safety, security can be quite an ephemeral thing. Helen Keller, while reflecting on her life without the aid of sight or sound, called security "Mostly a superstition that does not exist in nature, nor do the children of men as a whole experience it. To keep our faces toward change and behave like free spirits in the presence of fate is strength undefeatable. Life is either a daring adventure," she emphasized, "or nothing at all."

The need to control is dominated by the fear of loss. Although Bill and I thought we were willing to risk everything to achieve our dream, we were also trying to hold on to the outcome through our emotional attachment and fear of losing it. Like the monkey who refuses to release the food in its hand, we, too, can develop a form of paralysis and become our own captors through our refusal to let go. This hinders partnerships, destroys our vision and sense of purpose, and cuts off the creative process.

Chapter 7

Living in the Present

When I feel guilty over my imperfect past, or I am anxious over my unknown future, I do not live in the present. I experience pain. I make myself ill. And I am unhappy. My past was the present. And my future will be the present. The present moment is the only reality I ever experience. As long as I continue to stay in the present, I am happy forever: Because forever is always the present. The present is simply who I am, just the way I am—right now. And it is precious. I am precious. I am the precious present.

> **LIFE PRINCIPLE:**
>
> *Eternity is forever.
> Live this day the way
> you want to remember
> it tomorrow.*

—Spencer Johnson, MD,
The Precious Present

ALL THE PRINCIPLES I AM DISCUSSING have been available in various forms since the beginning of time to anyone who seeks them. We have been both admonished and promised that if we ask, it shall be given; if we knock, it shall be opened; if we seek, we will find. Everything we need for a rich and joyful life has been placed before us, yet seldom do we reach out and take what is already ours. If the principles for health, wealth, and happiness are there for the taking, why do we not reach out and gratefully partake of the banquet of life that is spread before us? Why aren't we disciplined, committed, purposeful, and living life fully? Why do we fail to seek, ask, and knock?

Life is rich and abundant, yet we often experience it as struggle and lack. The difficult problems of life can appear insurmountable. Somewhere along the way we lose our childlike expectancy and zest for living, and we give up large portions of who we really are. Disappointment, illness, and a sense of loss or impotence then become the common denominators of life. As Norman Cousins once observed, "The tragedy of life is not death, rather it is what we allow to die within us while we live."

The Human Camera

The world we see is just a projection of ourselves. As we play out our human drama, we become not only the camera but the writer, director, and editor. Philosophers through the ages have pointed out that there is a vast difference between the world of reality and our experience of it. No two of us (even if we have a twin) have exactly the same life experiences, nor do we receive and process information about our world in the same way. Much of our identity is formed by the early childhood decisions we made, the culture and roles we find ourselves in, and the expectations we strive to fulfill.

Consequently, each of us has developed a carefully constructed representation of the world that is not, in fact, reality. A representation is a model, not an actual manifestation. So without realizing it, a self-made model of reality determines our view of life. Like a human camera, we look through the distorted lens of our viewfinder and then project that view onto the world around us. This causes a distorted and impoverished view of reality, limiting our capacity for appropriate, spontaneous action.

A marvelous example of this surfaced several years ago in one of my Change Agent classes. The purpose of The Change Agent is to provide students with an opportunity for personal transformation by removing any barriers to living fully in the present and fulfilling their purpose as a leader. Two of the participants were Dawne and Jeanne, twin sisters who seemed to go out of their way to distinguish themselves from each other. One was a brunette, and the other was very blonde. One was

114

married, and one had remained single. One was shy and more intro-
verted; the other was vivacious and outgoing. Both, however, lived in
Atlanta, and both worked for the same large company that was partic-
ipating in the Learning Laboratories courses and seminars.

As part of their class assignment, students are asked to keep a
journal under the headings of events, feelings, reactions, and beliefs
to discover the people, places, or events that trigger certain emotions
and cause automatic, reactive thinking and behavior. Once this
awareness is in place, the student learns the art of Pause-a-tive-
ness—to pause before reacting to old stimuli in order to choose an
appropriate here-and-now response.

The weekend after receiving this assignment, both women went
to their parents' home for a visit. The next week in class, their jour-
nals looked something like this:

Dawne

Event—Went home for the weekend.
Feelings—Felt like a little girl again being under Mom and Dad's
    roof; uncertain of myself.
Reaction—Found it hard to tell them about my marriage and life.
Belief—No one really understands me or cares about my feelings.

Event—Went to the back yard and sat on the rock.
Feelings—Lonely, left out, sad.
Reaction—Lots of resistance and resentment toward Daddy and
    Jeanne.
Belief—If Daddy really loved me, he would have taken me to the
rock for long talks like he did Jeanne.

Jeanne

Event—Went home to see Mom, Dad, and my friends.
Feelings—Excited to see everyone.
Reaction—Called friends and planned a full weekend.
Belief—It's great to be back.

Event—Looked out the window and saw the rock.

Feelings—Anger, resentment.

Reaction—Wanted to get away, get out of the house.

Belief—It wasn't fair that Daddy always took me to the rock to scold me and not Dawne. Everything that happened was not my fault. No matter what I did or ever will do, it is not enough. I can never please him!

Very interesting! Twin sisters—same house, same parents, same places and events—yet two entirely different perceptions and reactions. Which one was right? Neither. Both were merely perspectives or points of view about "events" in their lives. They were perceptions of reality, and not reality itself. By definition, perception is "a specific idea, concept or impression," and it is a *mis*-perception—it's not the truth. And yet, this one issue—daddy and the rock—was the basis for long-held beliefs that triggered feelings of upset, unworthiness, and separation in both women.

The Principle of Pure Potential

In order to fully understand the process at work here, we need to have an accurate definition and model of our true nature and potential. The more we experience our true nature, the closer we come to the manifestation of our full potential. The root of the word *potent* is strength: that which has power. One empowering life principle operating in each of our lives is the law of pure potentiality. It states that our true nature is one of pure, limitless potential.

At birth, each of us is given a toolkit of five natural emotions: grief, anger, envy, fear, and love. These were designed as a means of appropriate expression in meeting the various challenges of life. Grief allows us to express sadness when we experience loss. Anger allows us to say "no" to people or activities that are counter to our values. Envy is a powerful motivator in the desire to strive harder and succeed. Natural fear builds caution into our nature and helps keep us safe and alive. Love is the highest form of emotion. When naturally and joyfully expressed, it is complete in itself. The problem arises when any of these natural emotions are thwarted or repressed and become distorted. In the extreme, the following can and often does occur:

Grief becomes chronic depression.

Anger becomes rage.

Envy becomes jealousy.

Fear becomes panic.

Love becomes possessiveness.

The following model was generated during my studies with Harvey Jackins (*The Human Side of Human Beings*) and during my involvement with Reevaluation Counseling in the early 1970s, and then further expanded and refined in the ensuing years. Through my work with private clients and thousands of Learning Laboratories students, I have had the opportunity to validate its usefulness with people from varying backgrounds and levels of success. This descriptive model explains the source and effect of early emotional damage and provides tools for tackling old, limiting thought and behavior patterns that keep us stuck in the past (which is fiction) and projecting into the future (which is prediction.)

The discussion that follows about the human difference, the effects of distress, and the storage of experience may not fit many of the things you have been taught to think about yourself or others, or the "way things are," and will likely require both critical thought and direct application. Our objective is to regain our full human potential by constructing a new, unique, accurate response to each new, unique moment of life. That's what is meant by living in the *now*.

It is clear that none of us ever confronts an "old" or identical situation. No identities in the physical universe—not even two electrons—are identical. Certainly anything as individual or complex as a personal experience will never be repeated exactly. Yet so often we find ourselves getting that "old feeling" or saying to ourselves, "Here we go again" or "Why does this keep happening to me?" In the case of Jeanne and Dawne, how could such unproductive feelings be triggered by merely going home for a visit? How could two such normally loving, intelligent, and capable people let something that occurred so long ago take control of their current spontaneity and happiness? What is the source of this apparently contradictory experience?

The Human Difference

All forms of life can be characterized by an active response to the environment, although plants and animals are limited by an inherited, restricted group of preset response patterns. In sharp contrast, nonliving matter is passive in response to its environment. If you move a chair, it stays moved. Its nature is to be "pushed around" rather than to "take charge."

The human difference is in the kind of active responses we make to our environment. Unlike the preset response patterns that limit other creatures, we possess a qualitatively different way of actively responding to our environment. This "human" ability allows us to create and use brand-new, unique responses in each new, unique situation we meet. When we are fully functioning in our distinctively human way, we do not have to use any previously worked-out responses. We are equipped to create responses that exactly match and successfully handle each new situation we confront throughout our lives. Our divine nature is to be creators, not reactors.

The failure to create and present such a new, unique, accurate response is set forth as an acquired, noninherent, and unnecessary human characteristic. The source of human irrationality is located in the early distress experiences we undergo and do not recover from completely. This results in limiting judgments, decisions, and beliefs we function out of and project onto everyday situations.

Unless we are born with damage to the forebrain, this special human ability or flexible "intelligence" is present in each one of us. Also present is a large, God-given capacity to choose our feelings, emotions, and attitudes, and the desire and ability to have warm, loving, cooperative relationships with others. In essence, this is who we are.

By now you may be thinking, "Who does she know that I don't know? This certainly does not match my experience of people or life!" And you are, unfortunately, correct. The flexible intelligence, the vast joy or zest for living, the ability to see each life situation uniquely and to respond appropriately is not abundantly evident. And we can't help but wonder, "What went wrong?"

The Effects of Distress

Given that the foregoing description of our God-given nature is valid, then obviously something has gone wrong. The failure to handle life situations well—whether making repetitive mistakes, blaming or finding fault with others, drowning in moods of depression, anxiety and guilt, or entanglement in miserable relationships—flows from one simple, common source: *We get hurt.* And while hurting (either physically or emotionally), our flexible human intelligence shuts down, although data continues to flow in through our senses of sight, touch, smell, taste, and sound.

We are all familiar with the following phrases that Harvey Jackins has used to describe the effects of a distress experience:

"I was scared out of my wits!"

"She was out of her mind with pain."

"He was so mad he couldn't hit the ground with his hat."

"She seemed to be in a fog for months after her mother died."

"You'd better take the rest of the day off. You're so upset, you'll only make mistakes anyway."

After a distressing experience, most of us assume we are soon over it and back on our feet again. This is what could and should take place, since information from a good experience is filed away as a resource for handling future situations. During a distress experience, however, information becomes misstored, jamming the system with unprocessed residue. This residue accumulates, much like scar tissue.

When we encounter this residue in a person's behavior or feelings, our impression is that the person has what we would call a rigid personality. If the behavior pattern has become so ingrained that any similarity to the old situation or feeling of hurt can cause it to be triggered (like Jeanne and Dawne with the rock), the pattern is chronic. Being stuck in a chronic pattern is like being trapped in an audible, steel cage that is constantly reminding you of some great perceived inadequacy. "You're so stupid!" it might say, or "I'm just not creative," or "I never could speak in front of a group of people," or "My dad is never going to let me grow up."

The Storage of Experience

So it is not just that we get hurt. What compounds it is that everything going on during that experience of hurt (the sights, sounds, physical sensations, etc.,) is literally being stored in the computer-with-memory-banks that is our brain. This was graphically demonstrated by a neurosurgeon named Penfield who found that the brain is similar to a high-fidelity tape recorder. When Penfield touched certain areas of the brain with electrodes, the person would not only remember specific events but would often remember and express the feeling that occurred at the time of those events.

From this, Penfield concluded that specific memories and emotions are recorded and stored and that they can be replayed today in as vivid a form as when they originally occurred. When aroused (or more accurately, restimulated) by current-day situations, the repressed emotions seem to apply to that event, although they really do not. In most cases, it is the old, accumulated emotions from childhood that are aroused. This explains why, as demonstrated in the case of Dawne and Jeanne, we often overreact to current-day situations. We are reacting not so much to current stresses (they were both looking forward to the trip home) as to the restimulated, repressed emotions from childhood.

Becoming Pause-a-tive Worksheet

The next time you find yourself emotionally triggered by a new (yet old) situation, take the opportunity to become Pause-a-tive by pausing to ask yourself these questions:

When have I felt this way before?

Who and what does this remind me of?

What did I do then? What did I decide?

As a result, how am I now behaving?

What generalizations or judgments have I made?

What beliefs have I developed?

How have these beliefs contributed to my view of life?

How are they limiting my thinking and behavior right now?

Anxiety from a current situation, if not handled appropriately, will either be stored in the body as stress, repressed into the subconscious, or projected as blame onto others. The thought "How could you/they do this to me!" is a sure indicator of self-victimization. Any form of blame simply leaves you unable to accept responsibility for, and thus powerless to correct, a situation. Yet this is precisely where the construction of a new, empowering model of reality must begin.

Who Do You Think You Are?

How we see ourselves is a matter of great importance. If I were to describe myself, the words might include child of God, woman, wife, mother, daughter, sister, friend, aunt, cousin, daughter-in-law, sister-in-law, writer, therapist, speaker, teacher, traveler, hostess, skier, creative, intuitive, purposeful, loving, committed, resilient, health-conscious, one who appreciates good wine, blue-eyed, etc.

Now—who do you think *you* are? What words describe *you* as you perceive yourself?

What words describe everything that is "Not you"—the people, places, and things you see, hear, feel, or sense that make up your world. These two areas combine to form your model of reality.

121

Most of us think of the words that describe "me" or "who I think I am" as our self-image. It is something we work very hard to develop, hone, protect, hang on to, and even defend. It seems very real, and we tend to think of it as *us*. Don't forget, however, that an image is merely an impression, representation, likeness, copy, or reflection of the real thing. It is not reality itself. Remember: a model, by definition, is simply a "representation" of something, and not the thing itself.

My purpose is to hold up a mirror so you can see the image for what it is: it is all your beliefs about who you are and who others are, and it comes from years of conditioning. Please notice the separateness that your image creates between you and everyone around you. If you are "me," then who or what is everything else? The answer can only be "not me," and thus the beginning of isolation and separateness.

Restrictive beliefs and patterns can have many deleterious effects on your behavior and experience of life. For instance, they can acutely limit your awareness of options or alternatives as an entrepreneur. If you "know" you can't do something, it will be difficult, if not impossible, for you to even consider another course of action, although it might be exactly the best thing to do. When you have a great deal at stake, you need to keep your thinking open and flexible, especially when it looks like you are being limited to one or no alternatives.

The thought that you are an isolated, separate entity prevents you from serving others and makes it impossible for them, or for Life, to serve you. Every organization I have ever worked with suffers from this perception. It is responsible for traditional organizational hierarchies and structures, and for the inability of one department or person to serve another. It produces divorce, divides cultures, and begets wars.

Trying to Figure Life Out

Our reaction to the so-called "events" of life, coupled with the decisions we make and the beliefs we hold so dear, creates inhibitors. And these inhibitors restrict our natural ability to demonstrate flexible intelligence, zestful enjoyment of living, and loving, cooperative relationships. Let's look further at the ways we can booby trap ourselves as we rationally try to process the people and events of our early lives.

Infants are powerful communicators. When they are wet, hungry, or experiencing any discomfort, they let us know in no uncertain terms—they cry. As parents, our job is to interpret those cries as accurately as possible and to provide nurture, comfort, and relief. Whether we are able to respond appropriately as adults depends a great deal on the way we were responded to as children, the decisions we made about ourselves, and the beliefs we now hold about parenting.

With an appropriate response to the child's cry, the system works perfectly to allow a sense of well-being, wholeness, or okayness. With an inappropriate response, such as irritation, upset, or anger, the system also works perfectly by providing feedback to the infant communicator. The problems occur in the interpretation of the feedback—what we think it means about them and what we think it means about us. Since our mind functions to give meaning to what it receives, it is constantly interpreting outside stimuli and filing it away for future reference.

Let's look more closely at how this works:

A child cries—to stay healthy and communicate.
An adult responds—to stop the crying and, hopefully, to fill the needs of the child.

A child crawls—to develop motor skills and explore her world.
An adult responds—to encourage or provide safety.

A child walks and reaches out—to explore and test his world.
An adult responds—to encourage the child and provide a safe environment.

A child talks and expresses emotions—to communicate and gain acceptance.
An adult reacts with parental messages—to stay comfortable and maintain control.

The system was designed perfectly—but what begins to happen? What mixed messages are starting to come across? What might the child decide they mean?

A child cries—An adult functions to stop the crying:
"What's the matter, sweetheart? What do you need?"
"Can't you keep that kid quiet?"
"There, there, don't cry. Here, this will make it better."
"Stop that crying, or I'll give you something to cry about!"
"Only babies cry."
Child's interpretation—It's not okay to express my feelings or be real.

A child walks or crawls—An adult encourages, but soon confines the child:
"Come on, come to mommy."
"That's my boy—look at those motor skills!"
"Into the playpen . . . mommy has work to do."
"Can't you ever sit still?"
"Why can't you be nice and quiet like your sister?"
Child's interpretation—Maybe it's not all right to explore and be curious.

A child talks or expresses emotions—An adult soon tries to maintain control:
"Say ma-ma, da-da. Listen—he's talking!"
"She has a very large vocabulary for a child her age."
"Doesn't that kid ever shut up?"
"Children are to be seen and not heard."
"Don't you talk back to me, young lady!"
Child's interpretation—I'd better not express myself.

The Problem of Being Okay

As children, we quickly learn that we didn't really see what we saw, we didn't really hear what we heard, we shouldn't really say what we think. In other words, we shouldn't be who we are. As we determine that being the way we are is *not okay*, we try to figure out how to act in order to *be* okay, and we start behaving according to that belief. Somewhere, underlying it all, is the sinister message, "You must . . . or else!" What is that thought for you? "I have to . . . or else." And thus a compulsive, inhibiting thought or behavior pattern is born that soon becomes a "truth."

In order to demonstrate how mixed up this whole process can become, I'll share with you what I did. I was born eighteen months after my sister, Michele, whom I adored. As we were growing up, I wanted to go where she went, do what she did, and look, dress, and act just like her. Our mother was disturbed by this because she knew that in a lot of ways Michele and I were not just alike (Michele has an olive complexion with hazel eyes, I'm fair-skinned with blue eyes), and she tried to dress us individually and encourage us to be ourselves. "You are not Michele," she told me. "You are Lauren. You are different, unique." Well, my little mind really went to work on *that* information!

First of all, Michele represented everything I wanted to be: she was pretty, smart, popular, and talented. Somehow, I figured out that if she was all that, and if I was different from her, it meant that I was none of those things. I thought she had a monopoly on all those qualities! So somewhere along the way, in order to solve the dilemma of "Who am I?" I decided to be "The one with the personality." Michele was the pianist—I became the actress.

The roles I assumed on stage allowed me to express those parts of me I so willingly gave up. However, I developed several limiting thoughts and behavior patterns that affected my grades, relationships, and overall well-being. I gave up the dream of being who I was and settled for a small piece of that potential. I even developed a life theme of "Oh, well!" Anytime I wanted to achieve something and was either afraid or disappointed, I would simply tell myself, "Oh, well—I didn't really want to do that anyway." Or because I had each of my high school years in a different city and school, I would rationalize, "Oh, well—I'm not going to be here much longer anyway."

Can you see what a horribly restrictive and compromising image I developed of myself? It permeated all aspects of my life. Except for speech, English, theater, acting, or other related areas I decided I owned, my grades were average and sometimes below average. Physically, I was very self-conscious and unsure of myself. Emotionally, I always felt like I was on the outside looking in, that I never quite belonged. I was a bulimic teenager (I thought I had invented it!) who sought to find herself in romantic novels and theatrical roles.

It wasn't until years later, when I discharged old hurts and dissolved old thought patterns, that I began to restructure my model of reality and empower myself as a beautiful, intelligent, purposeful, worthy, and loving person.

What Is Enough?

The main problem with deciding how we need to be in order to get by in life and then acting that way is trying to figure out *what is enough?* Even if I decide I can't win, there are other solutions:

I can please
I can rebel
I can go away
I can avoid loss

What will we do to be okay? Whatever we think it takes! Does any of it work? No, but we can pretend it does. Then, when faking it no longer works, we have a new problem: *If I can't win, how do I avoid losing?* There are several solutions to this one:

I can quit
I can be nice
I can become a problem
I can stop others from winning
I can play the game

I can destroy the game
I can be right and make others wrong
I can manipulate those around me
I can blame the circumstances of my life

We look everywhere—except within ourselves. We seek outside ourselves for new, more, different, better. This sets up a vicious circle of despair. This seeking of satisfaction merely results in more dissatisfaction.

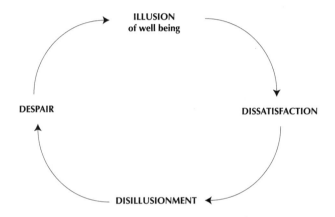

Since we have to put the blame somewhere, it looks like someone else (my mother!) did it to us, and we habitually seek to manipulate the people and circumstances around us. In the process, we develop reactive life positions such as striving, conforming, protecting, or becoming unaware.

Life Isn't Personal

We also tend to take things very personally. What my mother said to me wasn't personal. She just thought what she thought, and said what she said, out of her love for me and desire for me to be my unique self—and I took it personally. She would have done the same thing to any child who showed up looking like me and acting like me. And if we were to go to Dawne and Jeanne's father, asking him how he could have treated his daughters so badly, would he have any notion what we were talking about? Of course not! If we were to accuse my husband's uncle—who told him at his father's funeral when he was barely fourteen that he was now "the man of the family" for his mother and four sisters—of causing him to be a compulsive workaholic, he probably would have replied, "That's the way life is."

Any time you are off-purpose or not committed to your dream, you will find yourself striving to impress, convince, or overcome by strengthening and asserting your self-image. It is false security indeed to focus energy on something that doesn't even exist, something that, by definition, is not real.

Since image lives in the realm of ego, its aim is to look good and to protect and defend whom the ego thinks you are. It is based on fear and scarcity: either "I am not enough" or "There is not enough" (love, time, money, or things) to go around. Me-ism always creates problems: it keeps us victimized, powerless, and seeking or striving for more. It also destroys any possibility for authentic relationships. Our communications become full of deletions, distortions, and generalizations.

If the image you have of yourself is not real—if, in fact, it is not who you really are—what would that mean? If you are not your image, who are you?

Dismantling the Mask

Staying the way you decided to be in order to be okay is what image is all about. It is based on the illusion or concept called *me*. If we do receive acknowledgment or love, the fear that it is our act or pretense that is being validated can leave us feeling unfulfilled and dissatisfied. This is especially true for us entrepreneurs because we tend to accumulate and get caught up in the trappings of success. The enviable lifestyle we project makes it difficult for us to reveal—or for others even to believe—how devastating conditions can be during the bad times (few people had any idea what either our family or our business partner was going through). This causes us to withdraw into ourselves and tighten the mask we hide behind. Hiding to any degree keeps you emotionally stuck in the illusion of separateness from others. I often felt very isolated and lonely. Being authentic requires that we dismantle the mask. Any time you are feeling hurt, scared, and lonely, or you are suffering from impoverishment or depression, it is essential to develop a personal support system and a safe way to be vulnerable and real.

Here's the good news: you aren't who you think you are—you're not your perceptions or your self-image. The aspects of your model of reality that no longer serve you in fulfilling your dream can be dissolved, allowing you to recontextualize and transform (go beyond the form of) your life and construct new aspects that will enable you to create the future now. By letting go of the past, we discover the present, and the present is the only place we can live fully.

Lasting, constructive change begins on the inside and works its way out. One way to move out of the restrictive darkness of old, reactive patterns into the light of the present is by crystallizing and releasing the old hurts. The effects of these hurts has to come out some way, either though your change of mind, the tears from your eyes, or through a surgeon's scalpel. Breakdowns of any kind are over-accumulations in the reservoir of our mind or body. If the original hurt had been fully expressed and released at the time it happened, it would have emptied out and been filed away to serve as the basis for appropriate future action. But for most of us, this does not happen.

Any event that is experienced vividly in the imagination is stored as a "real" happening. That's why our hurts and distresses get locked in so deeply. Although attitude patterns and beliefs tend to be self-reinforcing (you know the management adage, "Make a decision, then make it right"), they can be changed. In the same way that you built your unique "reality" structure with your own thoughts and feelings, you can now restructure it through these same processes.

Suggested Assignment

I would like to suggest a way for you to see the pattern of events in your life over time and your resultant behavior that causes things in your life to keep repeating themselves. As you look at things over time, you begin to see patterns, ups and downs. Almost all your reactions now are to solutions to old problems that have created new problems. So the exercise is to chart the past events where you made up judgments and didn't tell the truth. (The truth believed is no longer simply the truth; that is, it becomes a belief that turns it into a position of right or wrong.) Truth can't be defended or sought. It can only be experienced in the moment called "Now."

Life Chart of Personal Time Histories

Look at your life, and chart it over time by writing about each of the key events or stepping stones. As you begin, it will all start coming back to you. Please pay particular attention to any areas you resist or don't want to deal with. Resistance is your shining star—it tells you where to go. Whatever we resist, persists in our lives. Using the following charts as guidelines, allow yourself to look a little deeper and determine the cause of that resistance.

What thoughts and feelings are being generated? With some places, you'll feel satisfaction; with others, you'll experience the pain.

Jot these down in a dialogue as you go, without judgments of right or wrong—no one was to blame. Just the facts: my energy was up, or was down; my relationship was together, or was falling apart; my love was freely given, or was withheld; etc. Notice how old patterns continue or flip over into your current life.

We often structure things to end up with what we don't want. But until we're aware of that negative pattern, we can't do anything about it. We have to identify it first. You can't do anything about a pattern when you're within the structure that caused the pattern in the first place—you can't talk yourself out of it, overcome it, positive think it, etc. However, patterns have modulation and frequencies. They oscillate and have peaks of waves. When you chart your life's events over time, you can actually see patterns and determine what's going on. You will be able to see yourself develop rigid ways of behaving, while others in the same event reacted quite differently, as in the case of Jeanne and Dawne discussed above.

Developing Your Life Chart

Since one of the best ways to let go of something is to see it over time, the following instructions will enable you to map out the model that causes stuck, repetitive, limiting thoughts and behaviors. Once you have done this, you will be able to tell the truth about them and make new, fundamental choices to reverse old patterns of behavior.

Although life is complex and never two-dimensional, we are setting this model up in a two-dimensional framework for ease of communication and understanding. To start, develop a two-dimensional chart such as the one illustrated below. As in the illustration, make the vertical bar in your chart go from low to high, and number it from 1 to 10. The area of 1 to 5 will be below a desirable level, and the 6 to 10 area will be positive, all the way up to your very best experiences.

Number the horizontal part of the chart in terms of years of your life or periods such as preschool, grade school, junior high, high school, college, work history, etc.

Then address each of the areas of your life that are fundamental to your success. Start with relationships. Begin with your parents, and then move to brothers and sisters, friends, teachers, authority figures, coaches, bosses, and then spouse, kids, direct family members, etc.

One way to view each category is to see hurts, conflicts, separation, distrust, any selfishness in the 1 to 5 area, and trust, love, sharing, intimacy, partnership, confidence in the 6 to 10 area.

As you go along and hit an emotional high or low point on the chart, make a note as to the event and what your judgment, decision, or reaction was, and how you (or they) behaved to prove yourself (or themselves) right and make others wrong.

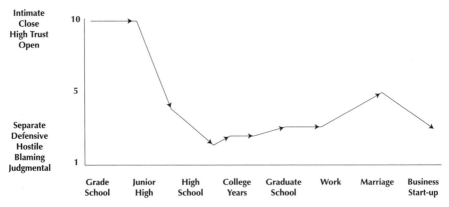

Examine your relationship with parents during the periods of your life.

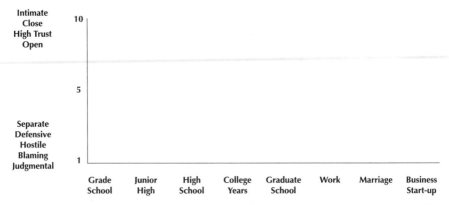

Examine your relationship with parents (or others) during the periods of your life.

Now, proceed with an examination of your physical self with another chart. Make 1 to 5 on the low end. During these low periods you may have had no energy, gained weight, smoked regularly, stopped exercising, abused alcohol or other drugs, neglected your appearance, etc. In the 6 to 10s, you were disciplined, worked out, followed a healthy diet, looked and felt great, etc.

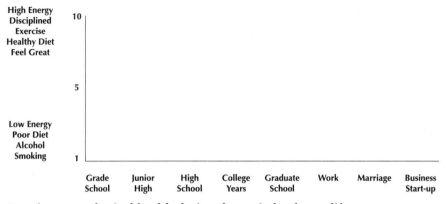

Examine your physical health during the periods of your life.

Then continue with a financial chart, with 1 to 5 being in debt or no savings and with 6 to 10 being increased earnings, savings, investments, etc. Note that 6 to 10 always requires effort, planning, goals, discipline, study, etc.

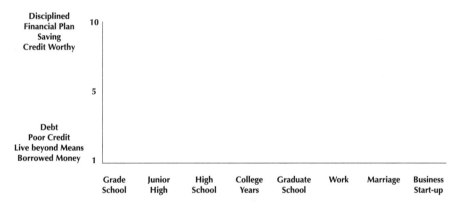

Examine your financial commitment & condition during the periods of your life.

Next, do an examination of your emotional state with another chart. You will see that it directly connects to all of the other charts.

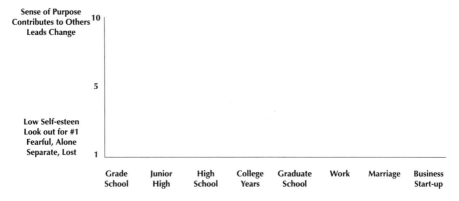

Examine your emotional health during the periods of your life.

Now make a chart to examine your relationship with God and your spiritual life.

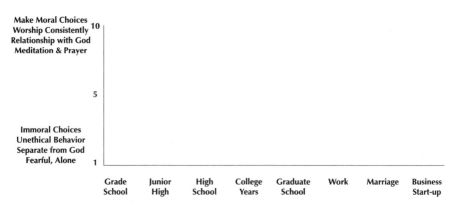

Examine your spiritual health during the periods of your live.

Next chart your intellectual growth. Challenge your depth of study, both formal and self-directed. Have you, every three years, developed expertise in some area? Are you considered by your peers to be of superior knowledge in specific areas of value? Do you stay up with the current thinking? Do you work to challenge and question things in order to grow?

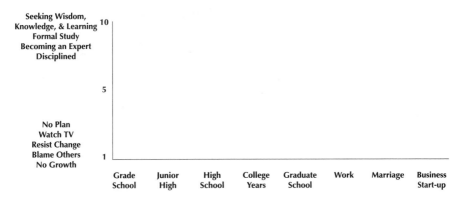

Examine your intellectual development during the periods of your life.

The last thing I would ask you to look at, though there are many other areas, is your contribution and service to others. Note that this requires your full attention. It is rare that you will engage in service to others unless all aspects of your life are in balance and doing well. If you are below the line (1 to 5) in any category, it is unlikely you will engage in fulfilling your life purpose of serving others. To truly serve others, you will need to be spiritually directed, intellectually capable of helping, caring in your relationships, feeling good physically, and strong emotionally.

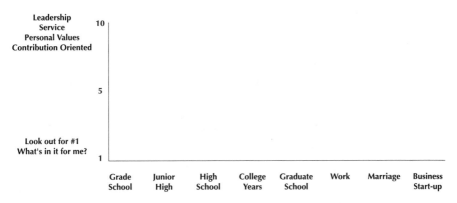

Examine your leadership and service during the periods of your life.

Now, examine the model of reality that caused you to believe that things were either high or low. Notice those beliefs that were due to what happened to you (an event) versus those in which you accomplished something due to a plan, disciplined action, or self-direction.

The universal model of reality for most people is based on the belief that something happened to them, "an event" took place. *It* happened to you. In the many years I have used this model to help others change, I have discovered that it doesn't matter whether the event was early sexual abuse or failure to receive a childhood desire, the judgment process was the same: You judged the event to be negative, not right, unfair, or bad, and you reacted strongly to it. And the others involved in the event reacted to your strong reaction, to which you reacted—making a self-regenerating, negative cycle.

Now here's the crux of the problem—In this reactive state, what decisions did you make? What actions did you take? How did your decisions, reactions, etc., contribute to a snowball or domino effect, thus amplifying the problem and making it worse? What effect does it have on your life and relationships, even today? What data have you gathered since that time to maintain your position that you were right and others or situations were wrong? How does this data contribute to the current belief about what happened to you? (By the way, these questions are applicable to both the 1 to 5 and 6 to 10 categories.)

Now notice how this model has actually contributed to your belief about everything that has ever happened in your life. How has it limited your development or led to periods of depression, upset, separation, anger, etc.?

Note that this model is one that causes you to not even want to get too excited or try something new and challenging because if you get too excited, intimate, or committed, you could get hurt again or experience the pain of failure.

To tell the truth is to see that you simply made up what happened by using this victim model of reality. You even formed your self-image based on this. You limited your life and shut down your real contribution to others. You constantly strove to seek another mode of happiness, finding it in food, sex, money, alcohol, etc. And then you experienced disappointment and eventual disillusionment with what you found. This model of seeking, finding, disappointment, disillusionment, and despair takes you all the way from a 10 to a 1 on your scale. None of it was real. All of it was based on a model that is not the truth! All of it is based on something or someone making you happy. It says your happiness is based on your model of reality. Not true!

Designing Your Future—Now

Now you can draw a line where you currently are in each of the life charts, and chart your future. Below it, note the fundamental choice you are making based on your life purpose. What is the discipline you are committed to following to make it real?

Step out in faith. See the resources around you when you commit to serve and fulfill your life purpose. Look at all feedback as working with you to make corrections and teach you what you need to learn. Open yourself up and celebrate the hurts and pain, knowing that you have placed yourself at risk and are stretching to learn and grow. This is almost as exhilarating as a little child learning to walk and discover the world in a totally new and exciting way. You are out of the restrictive victim model (baby playpen) and exploring the world from a completely transformed perspective. You now have a model that contributes to your (and others,) life in a powerful way. You are into responsibility management. You are in charge of your destiny and creating your future in the present. Congratulations! This is when you are most alive. This is what George Bernard Shaw meant when he spoke of "being a force of nature" or a "splendid torch" rather than a "feverish, selfish clod of ailments and grievances, complaining that the world will not devote itself to making you happy." Instead, you are being used for a noble purpose, secure in the knowledge that you are contributing to something bigger than yourself.

Empowering Your Imagination

Your point of view depends on your viewing point. Every thought felt to be true or allowed to be accepted as true in your conscious mind takes root in the subconscious mind and blossoms forth into like action. This is where commitment to your personal purpose comes in. It is the "inner movement of the heart" that counts.

The most important part of your reality is the emotional component. Positive thinking alone doesn't work. As we think in our hearts—our emotional center—so are we. Empowered imagination comes from the power of positive feeling! This implants the desire of your heart in your mind as though it is happening now. The chances are excellent that, in those areas where you are already succeeding and making the best use of your natural potential, you are already combining "*I am*" statements with vivid imagination.

The task now is to do it on a conscious, consistent basis.

The Triumph of the Human Spirit

When you change your beliefs, you change your life. Those of you who know either professional or Olympic athletes know they are highly conditioned to use the power of their imagination to practice their skills and build the confidence required to handle the pressures of intense competition. After Bill and I attended the 1996 Olympic Games in Atlanta, we witnessed an even more amazing celebration—the 1996 Paralympic Games—dedicated to "the triumph of the human spirit."

The gold round of the swimming finals was an unforgettable experience. If you have never seen the range of disabilities represented in the paralympic competitions, it is hard to comprehend what these athletes and their families must have overcome. There were swimmers with varying degrees of loss of sight. Swimmers with loss of limbs. Yet this was the happiest, most focused group I have ever seen. Every portion of an athlete's body that was not disabled was conditioned to perfection.

Can you imagine what was required to go from disbelief, hurt, anger, bitterness, discouragement, lack of purpose, or the lack of the will to live—to achieving the physique and mentality of a champion? Incredible! Before going into the water (some could only begin with an in-water start, not even a full dive), each competitor paused to concentrate, to mentally go over their performance. That moment's pause before starting the sequence of action was the last run-through in their heart and mind. The training and conditioning were there, yet the quality of the swim was as good as the athlete's ability to prime the system to do what it was prepared and trained to do.

More than 250 world records were broken during these Paralympic Games. What an astounding accomplishment! Banners everywhere asked those of us who were less physically challenged, "What's your excuse?"

My challenge to you is to let go of the past, discover the present, and live fully now. Discover the power of commitment, and allow yourself to be all used up today, not saving anything for tomorrow (which doesn't exist). There is nothing more to strive for or get to— all there is, is the precious present. It reveals everything you are and contains everything you need. So what's your excuse?

Chapter 8

Consciously Creating What You Want

Man is buffeted by circumstances so long as he believes himself to be the creature of outside conditions, but when he realizes that he is a creative power, and that he may command the hidden soil and seeds of his being out of which circumstances grow, he then becomes the rightful master of himself. Circumstance does not make the man; it reveals him to himself.

—James Allen, *As A Man Thinketh*

LIFE PRINCIPLE:

Our essential nature is pure creative consciousness.

That which is within you is unlimited and without form until you, through your imagination, call forth and bring into existence what you want. To be aware of this process is to be empowered.

—Terry Cole-Whittaker, *Having It All In a Have-Not World*

SUCCESSFUL ENTREPRENEURIAL LIVING demands a consciously creative mind. Once you have vision, you open yourself to the world of creation. This world is ruled by the structural principles of natural order. When you understand structure and its relationship to the creative process, you can purposely move from a lifetime of reacting to events, to the higher, realm of consciously creating the results

141

you want in your life. In addition, you will begin to create powerful partnerships that will naturally flow to you when you give to others what you want for yourself.

Although it's easy to rock along and take things for granted while the money is flowing, it is extremely difficult to activate or maintain the creative process when you're up against the wall—faced with making payroll, dealing with creditors, or frozen with the fear of not performing on a contract. All of a sudden, demands are coming at you from all directions. Your dream has become a nightmare. This can lead to panic, overreaction, and resorting to desperate measures.

It is at this very moment, however, that you can be your most creative self. You can become instantly resourceful, coming up with the ideas that will get you over the hump. This is the time for your people to pull together into a team as never before. Now your creativity must be at its highest, as well as your ability to see everything around you as a resource. Calls need to be made. But what do you say? What can you do to tap into this incredible power and keep from succumbing to reaction and fear?

Creating Dynamic Partnerships

Creative partnering is an arena where Bill and many of the entrepreneurs I know not only stay alive—it's where they actually thrive. Through an understanding of the power of creative thinking, they are able to form creative, dynamic partnerships. These synergistic relationships are developed by focusing on what the other person (your customer, vendor, supplier) needs and wants and figuring out how to give it to them. This skill is possible only when combined with the ability to build and maintain key relationships. This is where the creative process begins. Take the focus off yourself, your individual desperate condition, and think: "What do the people I need to do business with actually want? How do I give that to them through some form of win-win partnership?"

I will now give you some examples of how that can work.

In the case of CSTN, our business plan showed that we needed approximately $10,000,000 dollars to make it through the first couple of years and get "on the air." The first $300,000 came from personal consulting contracts we sold and fulfilled with twelve Atlanta firms. This executive alliance, known as the Executive Equation, served as a testing ground for our potential of team-based organizations. Each session revealed to us what the client organization needed next in order to continually better their past "best" performance. This information, along with some of their success stories, became training modules for the video satellite delivery we were going to offer. It also produced solid customer referrals when potential CSTN subscribers were checking out the Network.

After walking away from a potential investor, Bill made a list of what that money (if we had it) would have gone for. It included expanded office space, a video production studio with editing capabilities, a satellite uplink facility, securing transponders with unused satellite broadcast space (which was at a premium, since the one we were counting on became lost in space), the installation and maintenance of our subscribing clients' satellite dishes, the hiring of a marketing team and production crew, the actual production of enough video-based training programs (with their accompanying materials and workbooks) to fill an entire day of broadcast for five days a week, the ability to pay our high-profile faculty of consultants for their time and travel while making their training videos, our own travel expenses involved with marketing the concept and producing the programs, etc.

Bill first partnered with Dixieland Productions, where we were given space to build out and decorate a first-class headquarters as well as to use their high-end production facility. Bill, in turn, assisted Dixieland in developing and implementing a strategy to grow their business. They would also receive shares in our business, plus the duplication and distribution rights to our video programs.

It was discovered that GTE Spacenet had a new satellite that was being launched and was in need of a base client that would attract private satellite TV networks (K-band). With nothing but a dream,

Bill approached the CEO of GTE and walked out with the rights to what should have been a $150,000-a-month satellite transponder. We, in turn, brought private satellite networks to their transponder.

GTE also installed and maintained our subscribing clients' satellite dishes nationwide, plus they provided the financing for our contracts.

When we needed to be up on four satellites at a time for "The Quality Imperative" broadcast (narrowcast) to networks across the USA, Canada, and into South America, we partnered with Keystone Communications. Keystone also provided uplink studios on both the east and west coasts for the convenience of our faculty, while Bill, in turn, helped them to implement a strategic-growth strategy.

The composite value of this exchange of goods and services totaled close to $1,500,000 in actual out-of pocket cost, but over $4,000,000 in then-current market value.

Inventiveness abounded. By buying unused off-hour editing time (from 10 p.m. to 6 a.m.) at greatly reduced fees, we were able to accomplish for $30,000 what would have cost others $300,000. Borrowing from a Ben Franklin quote, "If a man could have half his wishes, he would double his troubles." I can't help thinking that, if we had actually secured up-front the $10,000,000 we thought we needed to get started, it probably would have cost us twice that amount! Not having that money spurred the creative efforts of everyone around us. If we had had the money to accomplish all of this, the creative process would never have been so powerful.

Since we could not offer appropriate salaries and benefits, each team member came on board out of their desire to contribute rather than just to show up and collect a paycheck. Out of their commitment to the dream, vice-presidents Walter Snead and Jerry Gardner contributed substantial personal funds. As Vice-president of Engineering, Walt worked months without pay, funding corporate travel and other purchases on his and his wife Susan's personal credit cards when ours were cut off. Three of our most capable staff members, Linda Vephula, Lois Guilbeau, and Jan Flint, worked long, dedicated hours for significantly less than their real value in a normal job market. People showed up on our doorstep, offering to contribute months of their time and talents in creative and computer-related areas. Randy Rivers, a talented director, editor, and cameraman, followed us to Atlanta from Florida with his bride, Susan, with few financial guarantees.

And then there was the CSTN faculty, which consisted of some of the finest minds in the business world. These in-demand, highly paid authorities contributed hours of their time developing a video-based format for their teachings. They often paid their own hotel and travel expenses while going from site to site taping documentaries of their groundbreaking work with clients. Some hired writers to work on their workbooks and, in one case, put the entire TV crew up in their home while we shot their programming on the west coast. These efforts bridged the gap in active marketing created by the lengthy fund-raising period, and funded the development of a $3,000,000 inventory of Total Quality Management video programming and printed course materials.

These are just some of the highlights. I will mention two creative solutions to our own personal travel needs. On several occasions, Bill and I needed to travel from our live teleconference in Washington, D.C., to other commitments in New York City. We saved hundred of dollars in hotel and air fare by booking a sleeper on the Washington-New York rail line. This allowed us to board in the evening and spend the night on the train, since it did not arrive in New York City until the next morning. And when we made the moves to and from Florida, Walt Snead found a large commercial transport truck going our way that had extra space. The trucker charged a fraction of the cost of a moving van.

The Creatively Challenged

Since it is through the power of our creative imagination that we can dream a dream or solve a problem, this poses a challenge for the majority of us who, through some unnatural thwarting at an early age, decided we were neither creative nor artistic nor imaginative.

Although I don't consciously remember the event that caused it, I do know that my own artistic development ceased around the third grade. The only pictures I attempted to draw after that time were based on the primitive, childish renderings I had perfected by then. One was a pond and a tree on a grassy knoll. The tree had roots, branches, and leaves. The pond had ripples and ducks. V-shaped birds flew in the blue sky. The other featured a teepee on another grassy knoll. The teepee was covered with various insignia which, I imagined, were representative of American Indian life and culture: a sun, a moon, ripples of water, V-shaped birds, stick people and animals, etc. It was not until my late thirties, while studying briefly with the brilliant artist, Paul Chelko, that I developed the ability to see beyond those crippling self-limits through the use of mental pictures and the laws of creative thought.

Thoughts are powerful things. Remember that our dominating thoughts, when mixed with definiteness of purpose and a burning desire, will eventually be achieved. This is a law of life. Many who have succeeded in life have overcome multiple setbacks and heartbreaks because they understood and used (whether consciously or unconsciously) the laws of the creative process to fulfill their life's dream.

Since everything we see around us was at one time just a thought, it follows that all creation begins with thought. Thought is pure energy. In other words, everything that exists in our lives, whether we consider it positive or negative, is created by our thoughts. Thoughts are things. They are somewhat random until they are experienced on a deep, feeling level. From there, they are formed into thought patterns and beliefs. Then they become programs, paradigms, or preconceived ideas from which we interpret the world around us, determining how we react or behave. As we change our thoughts, we change our world, and thus the quality of our lives. Creativity—for each of us—can be as simple as a new way of seeing what already exists.

Think about what can be generated when we choose to view the power of thought in this way. Does this mean that we personally attract the people and create the circumstances around us? It most

146

certainly does. But how could this be possible when we don't even want or like so much of what we have and see? This is not only possible, but it is an amazingly common phenomenon. Since energy attracts like energy, what we fear, for instance, is what we attract. The correction process proceeds only from an understanding of both the properties and potential uses of our creative energy.

All Things Are Energy

Energy is available to each of us all of the time, in limitless supply. With the intelligence of God behind it, the flow of energy is determined by very specific laws. This energy occurs in two states: manifest thought energy (all things in solid form) and unmanifest energy, thoughts or ideas that we have not yet released. In truth, even those objects that seem most solid to the naked eye, such as buildings or trees, appear as molecules in motion when viewed under high power microscopes. And the mechanism that causes this energy to reach its materialized form is simply—thought.

This God-given power has absolutely no limits placed upon it. And since we are thinking all the time, this means we are consistently living in a creative state, influencing energy all of the time. Pretty exciting stuff! Emotion is energy in motion. Our intense feelings in a state of emotional awareness are what give our thoughts their power. Our responsibility in fully availing ourselves of this creative power is to first believe in it and, more important to use it in only purposeful ways.

Understanding Structure

A good deal of the work Bill does with executive groups is based on the principles of System Dynamics. In a way that is similar to your charting life events, Bill has the organizations he works with develop time histories by charting their organizational events. His overall objective is to clearly reveal the hidden, underlying structure of the organization that causes the repetitive patterns and mistakes that management teams are constantly reacting to. Does it surprise you to learn that organizations have an unseen, underlying structure? In reality, all things have an underlying, unifying structure that determines how they function. Understanding structure allows you to make the shift from old, reactive patterns to fully unleashing your creative power. That's why we're going to focus for a moment on structural thinking.

Structure represents the way something is constructed or put together. The following insights taken from the physical world can serve as a catalyst for creative change to take place in your life:

1. Everything takes the path of least resistance. Water moves where it is easiest for it to go. Human energy is like a river that flows through life, always taking the path of least resistance. This is an important concept because wherever you are in life right now was determined by, and is a result of, the path of least resistance you have previously taken.

2. The path of least resistance is determined by the underlying structure. Although the water moves according to the land's structure (where it is easiest for it to go), the structure of the land remains the same, whether there is water flowing through it or not. Old man river has been flowing for a long time, even though he may periodically dry up or change with the seasons. Therefore, though it may periodically seem as though you have changed—or things are better—because someone or something is different (new client/boss, a bank loan, weight loss, etc.), this is only a change in appearance. You have not changed your life unless the fundamental underlying structure has changed.

3. You can, however, change the basic structures of your life. The new path causes the river to naturally surge toward the life you want. In other words, you have the ability to determine the river's flow (and thus the path of least resistance) much as an engineer does when altering a riverbed.

4. To make any shift, you must first determine your starting point. For many people, that means a life position of reacting to events from the past (which didn't really happen) or projecting them into the future. In either of these positions, the path of least resistance can only lead to unwanted outcomes. Then it seems that circumstances are more powerful than you are. As long as your life structure remains unchanged, you will tend to gravitate back to old familiar patterns—no matter how much you really want to change your life, and no matter how hard you try.

Generally, we believe that if circumstances would somehow change—"if only . . ." would happen, or if only we had more . . . (money, time, love, etc.)—we would be able to function happily and effectively and have a fulfilling life. This is the Be-Do-Have paradigm. In actuality, it is the "being" of something that produces the "having." By sincerely acting as if you already are what you wish to be, you draw it to you.

As long as it seems that power lies in outside circumstances, no matter what the outcome or success, there is a feeling of incompleteness and dissatisfaction. Success becomes an empty victory. It looks as if life is a certain way and we can't change it, no matter how hard we try, so we'd better negotiate around it. This keeps us stuck in a powerless, victim-based position that can be characterized by various behavioral strategies such as withdrawal, passive aggression, compromise, or the employment of pre-emptive strikes.

It is impossible to make changes from within what Robert Fritz, in his book, *The Path of Least Resistance*, calls the reactive-responsive orientation—because you are in a closed, circular system. "If you attempt to solve, change, break through, transform, accept, reject or avoid this structure, all you will do is reinforce it," he admonishes. So as common sense would dictate, when you find yourself in a hole, stop digging. This is the point at which your personal purpose becomes your lifeline. It's your way out of the hole. With your focus principle-centered and firmly fixed on your vision, values, and purpose, you place yourself in the position to make a successful shift to a new orientation.

The Shift

Once we are oriented in the creative process, we can move from a reactive to a consciously creative mode. When you shift from reacting to creating, the path of least resistance is directed toward specific, chosen results. The focus is then on what you want rather than on what you don't want. In the words of Robert Fritz, "you establish a new bond between you as creator and reality as your field of creation. The result is a reuniting with the power of the individual and a renewal of the human spirit." Fritz relates, "Over and over again I have seen people, when reunited with their power to create, aspire to what is highest in humanity: freedom, justice, peace, love, purpose, truth. No one tells them that these are the values to which they should aspire. These values emanate from what they truly care about."

As you develop new structures, results that may have seemed impossible or elusive in the past can now be created almost effortlessly. The key element required to make the shift from reactive to creative is the structural tension that is generated by the natural movement of tension toward resolution, like the compressed coil of a spring. This is similar to what is sometimes referred to as cognitive dissonance—the acute discrepancy between the way things are and the way we would like them to be. This restless urge for something better has been referred to as the mark of the artist or saint. The natural emotion of envy can help to bring this about by making us continue to strive for what we want. When we envy or wish to emulate someone, we create structural tension. As tension moves toward resolution, energy is released.

There are two components in creating the structural tension that will propel you to a breakthrough level of achievement: Vision of what you want, and a clear picture of your current reality (what you now have).

The difference between your dream and your current reality (cognitive dissonance) creates structural tension. This is the source of enormous power and energy since the path of least resistance is structured to resolve the discrepancy in favor of the vision. This is because your creative subconscious seeks to resolve the conflict in the direction of the strongest picture or image. Since tension strives for resolution, this discrepancy is to be cultivated, rather than avoided. Just as the structural tendency of a stretched rubber band is to move from being stretched to being relaxed, the structural tendency to move toward your end desire is now the direction that the path of least resistance tends to take.

Creation is manifest out of intention. When your thoughts, feelings, words, and actions are aligned with your purposeful intention, they restructure your mental and physical worlds in alignment with your spiritual world, producing the best possible results.

One caveat: cultivating intense, purposeful desire for something is not the same as being ruled by your everyday feelings. It is unwise to allow those feelings to become the standard of measurement of how you are doing in life.

Some people, despite what is actually taking place, think that if they are feeling uncomfortable, they are not doing well. For those of you who are on the entrepreneurial path (which is seldom comfortable), this type of distortion can become deadly. Feelings are in a constant state of flux, so the danger here is that when your emotions become the barometer in your life, your experience of life is determined by "How do I feel?" and not "What do I truly want?" It can be an insidious trap, since long-term successful living demands a commitment to doing that which is right or purposeful for our highest good, rather than what we feel like doing at the moment.

Mastering the Creative Process

The creative process is an exact replication of the human birth cycle. In fact, all complete creative processes move through this cycle, whether you are growing a garden or a business. Germination is the period in which something (the seed) can be planted and grown. I've heard it described as "the impulse that sets creation in movement." This is the prime initiation stage, when vision, enthusiasm, insight, and energy abound for your business or project.

The second step is absorption. This stage of development is particularly subtle because the germinal idea is still taking root, primarily drawing upon your inner resources. This phase requires a deep appreciation for time delays. Yet as you step forth with both inner force and outer action, you begin to generate momentum. The path of least resistance now leads toward the business or project having form and becoming a viable entity, thanks to some structural changes.

With fruition, you achieve what you have desired and worked for. You have earned the supreme enjoyment and possession of your heart's desire as you begin to receive the fruits of your endeavors. Receiving is an essential phase of creation, yet some people are uncomfortable with actually getting what they want. For instance, the majority of entrepreneurs get stuck in the survival aspects of the absorption process and fail to bring their vision to fruition. Many artists and writers fall just short of completing their works. Fulfillment somehow symbolizes loss. Without fruition, there is no contribution and no opportunity for celebration. And without the energy of completion, it is difficult to move on to a new creative vision and a new germination cycle. Completion compels you to move forward.

The Power of Choice

When the question arises "How do I know what I want to create?" finding the answer is the fun part. You get to make it up! Then the discrepancy between your current reality and the goals you vividly and passionately envision for your life serves as the structural tension to propel you forward.

Creative energy is wonderfully exponential in nature. You activate the seeds of your creation by choosing the results you want to produce. Contextually, deciding to do something is not the same as choosing to do it. The root of *decide* is the same as homicide and suicide, meaning to kill or cut off. By definition, it is limiting. We usually decide something by a process of elimination, for example, "Well, I sure don't want to do that." Not having what you want is a fairly good indicator that you are not choosing it.

To choose is to select something by preference, out of your vision, formally declaring the desired result. The intense desire or wish for something, as you will recall, is the activating force for germination. Choice is power. "How do I choose to live my life?" "Who do I choose to be?" Everything of consequence in your life is determined by your answer to this question—What is your choice?

Whatever you choose to do, allow yourself to enjoy it fully. When determining what you truly want, *think big*. Your mind doesn't know the difference! It tries to determine what you want by what you say you don't want because you've programmed it that way through a lifetime of taking the path of least resistance. And it thinks its job is to protect you from what you don't want. Instead, it must be trained to focus only on what you do want.

"What do I want?" This is the first question of the creative process, and you are the only one who knows the answer. Notice, however, that as soon as you ask yourself that question, resistance comes up, along with all the reasons you think you can't. The reason most people are unwilling to focus on what they truly want is twofold:

1. The fear of failure. Fear is what Carlos Castaneda's Don Juan called "the first enemy." Whatever you want to do will have not only an element of the unknown but also a new and scary feeling of being highly visible. Any personal growth or change requires you to be vulnerable, and it may feel like your self-image, and even your dream, is at stake. There is only one way to stay free of fear—remain paralyzed in the comfortable and deadening boredom of the known.

2. The fear of risk. Declaring what you want looks risky: you may mess up, get hurt, look foolish, or find out that you're not qualified. To actually get what you want is to face another unknown: things won't be the same. This can represent potential loss because the known—no matter how bad it is—is more comfortable to some people than the unknown. Going for it all requires a commitment to commitment.

When you doubt your abilities or question whether you deserve to have and produce whatever you want for yourself, "What do I want?" can be an overwhelming question. I can remember when I first wanted to teach on the university level but wasn't sure I was "ready." I kept waiting for someone to come along and "knight me," or bestow the power upon me to do what I wanted. This caused me to hesitate to put myself out there and delayed making it happen.

Any external search for the answer, rather than looking within, will have you stuck in the reactive mode, constantly searching for approval or waiting for something you think you need in order to get on with your life. If you dwell on the question "But how am I going to get there?" you are in danger of getting stuck in the process rather than staying focused on the desired result until completion.

Worksheet for Conscious Creation

Consciously creating what you want is diametrically opposed to taking the path of least resistance, or going along to see what life dishes out. The three God-given tools of creation are *thought, word,* and *action.* The following steps will put the tools to work and lead you to success.

Step 1. Go back to your purpose statement so that you are consciously focused in thought on who you are and your chosen function in life. Give your word by writing it down.

Step 2. With that thought in mind, further declare your word by writing down exactly what you want. Be specific. Be willing to expand your thinking. By willing, I mean, how much good are you willing to allow in your life? How big a contribution are you willing to make? (Terry Cole-Whittaker, in her book *Having It All In a Have-Not World,* suggests looking at beautiful things or qualities of life and saying, "I can have that," or, "Wow! That's for me," or, "It's okay for me to have exactly what I want. Everything in life is here for me to enjoy.")

Step 3. Set a target date. Then structure the steps to your goal on a simple flow chart.

Step 4. Take action by being prepared. If your vision and desire are bigger than your knowledge, skills, or experience, immerse yourself in the information. When Bill first conceived of CSTN, he knew nothing about satellite technology—he could barely operate a VCR. He devoted months to becoming an expert in the field. Talk to others.

Get advice and practical instruction. If appropriate, rehearse what you are going to say.

Step 5. As you step out by putting your knowledge and faith into action, focus your attention on your purposeful task and away from yourself. It's better to make some mistakes along the way than to stop for fear of making them.

Step 6. Celebrate every victory! With completion comes celebration.

Living on the Edge

As entrepreneurs, our family learned to live on the edge of life. This required us to restructure our lives so that the path of least resistance became the path to our dreams. You do the same. Let the structural tension that exists between where you now stand and where you want to go propel you in that direction. Now might be a good time to remind yourself of all the resources that are waiting for you to step out in faith through committed action.

"When the artist is alive in any person," writes Robert Henri in *The Art Of Spirit*, "whatever his kind of work may be, he becomes an inventive, searching, daring, self-expressing creature." Doesn't that sound like the real you? Out of the depths of your imagination, unlimited by your past, your belief systems, or your current conditions, *you* are the source of fulfillment for the daring of your imagination!

Chapter 9

Developing Perspective and Life Balance

There's nothing good or bad but thinking makes it so.

—William Shakespeare

Healthy people are beautiful people. Perhaps by standards of glamour they may not have completely regular features or proportions, but their eyes are bright, their hair shines, and their skin is clear. They stand

---

LIFE PRINCIPLE:

We have been given dominion over all things.

---

erect and walk with graceful stride. They can work hard and play hard. They know the real joy of living. They awaken rested and filled with anticipation. They meet the challenges of each day happily with clean, keen minds. They sleep peacefully without artificial aids.

Healthy persons are likely to be successful. They make a good impression on others. They learn well, make good use of available time, are dependable and good stewards.

—Mildred Nelson Smith, *The Word of Wisdom...Principle with Promise*

MAINTAINING THE WHOLENESS OF LIFE CAN BE DIFFICULT. When the economic future of your family and organization is dependent on your time, talents, and ingenuity, it may seem impossible to achieve any perspective, balance, or control. It is then that we become vulnerable to the three crippling afflictions of fragmentation, burnout, and overwhelm. Any one of these can take its toll on your emotional, physical, and spiritual well-being.

The multiple, accumulated demands on our time and energy can result in a feeling of being isolated, strung out, and scattered into broken, jagged pieces. Fragmentation not only leaves us physically weary and emotionally fragile, but it destroys the soul. We begin to lose the big picture, our vision of the future, and our sense of purpose.

Burnout is characterized by the loss of energy and commitment that comes to those who labor under stress without recreation, rest, and spiritual renewal. It attacks when we give unstintingly of our time and ourselves without receiving compensating care and nourishment. The struggle for survival can keep us so one-dimensional that we lose all balance. At such times, it's hard to remember that even God allowed himself a day of rest!

Either fragmentation or burnout can lead to a sense of deep emotional overwhelm and crushing powerlessness. What really exhausted Bill was the overwhelming responsibility he felt for the support and livelihood of our staff and employees. The mornings I awoke hearing his deep, anguished sighs are indelibly imprinted on my mind. Those of you who have had the experience of not being able to meet payroll, or suffer from the fear of that happening, will understand what a horribly disempowering experience that can be.

Whenever we look at our life experiences, it is common to label them as either good or bad. Yet the perception of good and bad events is an illusion. There really are no events at all. What we think of as an event is simply an accumulation that finally gets our attention. All our experiences, when looked at over time, are simply phases of life that oscillate to an increasing or decreasing degree. I was fascinated to discover that the Chinese symbol for the word *crisis* and the word *choice* are the same. Poignantly, the same symbol implies both *danger* and *opportunity*.

Ben Franklin has been quoted as saying, "If man could have half his wishes he would double his trouble." Many of our desires, if they were immediately gratified, would be disastrous in results. And often, when we have the greatest abundance in our lives, we make the worst mistakes. When we have less, we often make higher quality decisions and use our resources more effectively because we have nowhere to go but forward. The key is not to think "This is terrible" or "This is great!" It is what it is. What is crucial is that you seek to live your life according to the same principles, regardless of the circumstances— particularly under extreme duress.

Few chosen lifestyles present a greater challenge than that of the entrepreneur. If there is one word that most aptly describes the entrepreneurial life, I think it is mercurial—quick, volatile, changeable, fickle—derived from the Greek god of commerce, Mercury. The word, by definition, implies high risk. So it is natural that, when groups of entrepreneurs or their families get together, they swap horror stories. "You think that was bad," someone will say, "wait until you hear what happened to us!" In the hope of adding some perspective to whatever you are currently going through, I'll share a couple of my favorites by starting with one of my own worst-case scenarios. Talk about an accumulation!

At the height of our most difficult financial period, I was in an almost constant state of tension. I began trying to hold myself together any way possible. I was drinking cups and cups of coffee each day, and several glasses of wine at night. I got very little exercise. I was eating whatever was handy or available during the day, including lots of free (mostly fried) hor'dourves at the Buckhead Club for dinner. After a few more hours of work, I'd go home and, if I wasn't too numb, have a good cry. In the mornings, I could barely drag myself out of bed.

One evening early in December 1989, I felt a "zing" in my breast, and a lump the size of a golf ball suddenly appeared. At first, it was more shocking than frightening, but it couldn't have come at a worse time. Things were terribly tight. Our insurance had been canceled. I was feeling a great deal of stress. Our management team was surviving on a hopeful, day-to-day basis while the signing of a new, major contract kept being delayed. Debt and internal tensions were accelerating. Suddenly one day, I had had it! I was done—I was through! I no longer cared, and I wanted out!

I stayed home for days, feeling desperate and depressed, not getting dressed or caring how I looked. One afternoon, at the height of all this, I was talking on the phone to a former client and friend who had generously loaned us his home equity funds and now had an imminent need to get them back. Suddenly, my computerized phone went dead. I was already feeling a little crazy, and this put me over the top.

I ran to the door and out onto the front deck where I saw two men casually walking toward the street from the side of our house. Like a rabid banshee, I screamed at them, "What do you think you're doing?"

"We've just cut off your electricity, ma'am," they calmly replied.

"You can't do that," I yelled, "We have until five o'clock to pay that bill! It's only three! Here I am home from work—dying of cancer—and you have the nerve to jeopardize my health this way. I can't stand any more stress!"

As they quietly conferred with each other, I noticed that one of my more sophisticated neighbors, Millie, was jogging by, taking in the entire scene.

The men must have decided I was potential-for-lawsuit material. They said that, under the circumstances, they would turn our power back on until 5:00 p.m.

I stormed back into the house and called the office. Crying hysterically, I ordered someone to "Get that damn bill paid right now!" Thankfully, somehow it was.

Looking back, I realize the truth stated in the following quote by a brilliant and controversial general of the United States Army, Douglas MacArthur:

> In the central place of every heart there is
> a recording chamber. So long as it receives
> a message of beauty, hope, cheer, and
> courage—so long are you young. When
> the wires are all down and our heart is

160

*covered with the snow of pessimism and
the ice of cynicism, then, and only then,
are you grown old.*

That's exactly what happened to me—the wires were, literally, all down, my heart was covered with icy pessimism and hardened by cynicism. And I looked and felt very, very old. It was one of the worst days of my life.

Life on the Edge

A dear friend, Susan Carey, wife of top-gun pilot and daring entrepreneur Max Carey, told me this story. We were seated in the enormous master bedroom suite of their spacious Atlanta home, having a cup of tea beside a cozy fire, when I asked her, "How bad did it get?"

She laughed softly, then said, "It's like—if it isn't difficult, Max isn't comfortable! He lives every day on the edge, and as soon as things get comfortable, he steps out again." She paused to think before she continued.

"I remember a particularly bad period. For about two years, I was in a deep depression. This was related to the fact that our marriage was very troubled. The place where we lived was horrible, we were in terrible financial stress, our car was being repossessed, and we were four months behind on our mortgage payments—not to mention how many times rude bill collectors verbally accosted me. We had two pre-schoolers in diapers, no money for groceries, and maybe $35 for the whole week—it was just awful.

"When we got down to nothing, I would call my mom and ask her to lend me fifty bucks, or maybe a hundred. I'd go to the store every day with five dollars, or whatever, and I'd get chicken, or potatoes, or something like that. Back home, I'd make chicken 'whatever' or big pots of spaghetti. I don't know how we managed as well as we did because we couldn't pay a lot of our bills!

"One of my most vivid recollections," Susan said, smiling at the memory, "is the morning Max was in the shower when our water got

161

turned off. He came bursting out with soap in his hair, dripping onto his face. He grabbed a towel, and went running down the street yelling and chasing after the water man, wearing nothing but the towel!"

We both laughed. Then I asked about their three children, Billy, Elise and Caroline. "What did you tell the kids about what was going on, and how did it effect them?"

"When things were the worst," Susan replied, "they were still very little—but we did have to talk about it some. When Elise was in kindergarten or first grade, the colored Izod shirts were in. She wanted an Izod shirt more than anything. It was $15.95, and I didn't have $15.95. All her friends had them in every color, and she desperately wanted one. And, as you know from having your children, it broke my heart. Most of her friends had at least three or four; I wanted so badly to get her just one. I remember how thrilled we were when we were finally able to buy that shirt! It was pink, and she wore it every other day to school." Stoking the fire, Susan continued, "I think it really meant a lot to her—it was even more special—because she knew how difficult it was for us to give it to her."

Managing the Things You Can Control

Although the comfort zone for most entrepreneurs is to feel in control, it constantly surprises me how little control any of us have. That's why I think it's important to assess the things you actually can control, and to manage them the best way you can. The only thing I have ever had any control over is, myself—what I thought, how I felt, how I looked, and what went into and came out of my mouth. That's about it. And as the above and the following scenario demonstrate, I haven't always been able to master that.

Practicing Personal Stewardship

I believe, however, that each of us has personal stewardship responsibility to care for whatever is in our trust to the best of our ability. Stewardship is vast in scope, encompassing all of life. It covers all things—not only tangibles such as our bodies, home, children, parents, friends, or money, but also the intangibles, such as the use of our hearts, minds, and talents. We are called to care for them, to expand and extend their usefulness, and to use them in furthering our purpose here on earth. The thought that whatever we possess is "ours" goes contrary to the principle of stewardship. A steward is someone who manages someone else's property, finances, or other affairs. God has entrusted His earthly resources to us to manage for His purposes.

Taking Care of Yourself and Those You Love

Not quite a year after I successfully and nonsurgically dissolved the golf-ball-sized lump in my breast (through nutrition, an abrupt change in lifestyle, and decreased levels of stress), I discovered another smaller one in my other breast. This time I was really scared, and the lump definitely had my full attention. I wanted to do everything in my power to mobilize my body's own healing powers and strengthen it for whatever was ahead.

It is not that I didn't know better about taking care of my health during the time I was feeling the stress of launching our new global business; I had taken an active, preventive approach to health for years. My father was one of the original "health nuts." By the time I was fifteen years old, he was very well read in all the early research and studies of natural or holistic health. We all drank apple cider vinegar and honey "tonics." He personally ground the whole wheat for our morning pancakes. He was a great believer in the value of Vitamin E for a strong, healthy heart, and an early user of the chiropractic approach for preventive health.

In addition, Bill and I have long shared a common interest in preventative, nonmedical approaches to high energy, longevity, and health. Even before we met, we were familiar with the Edgar Cayce studies, and we both had successful experiences with chiropractics. Throughout the Learning Laboratories years, we consulted with and learned from many top experts in various fields of health, bringing them or their teachings to our students. We habitually get aerobic exercise, fast on a quarterly basis, and do an annual cleansing of the colon. (What an eye opener that is!)

Meanwhile, during the year after my first lump "poofed," I slowly slipped back into the deadly habit of knowing but not doing. My jogging stopped, and indiscriminate eating and drinking crept in. Once again, I allowed myself to become tense, isolated, and emotionally fragile. Thus, the inevitable happened.

One morning, as I lay in bed doing a breast self-exam, I discovered a hard lump. My immediate thought was, "You've broken the rules, and this is the consequence." I felt sure that it was cancerous. And once again, that thought mobilized me into action. Knowing how strong the mind-body connection is, I felt a very real responsibility for what had happened. I also determined to do everything in my power to naturally correct and strengthen my immune system before turning myself over to the "cut and drug" approach of traditional medicine.

I began reading everything I could get my hands on about cancer. I researched which foods had specific healing properties. I consulted several experts and teachers of preventative approaches to health. Each of them emphasized the strong connection between emotional, spiritual, and physical wellness, and the devastating exaction stress can place on all of these areas. I also learned that when these are in balance, our brain registers good feelings and triggers the rest of the body to feel good. When the body gets the message, the brain starts manufacturing a natural chemical called serotonin, often referred to as the body's "natural healer." This acts as a tranquilizer, soothing the body's cells—particularity those that make up the immune system, strengthening it so it can do its job and fight off disease.

To help establish this balance, I ran or fast-walked faithfully. As I did so, I told myself over and over, "Cancer cannot live in an oxygenated body, cancer cannot live in an oxygenated body." I used that time outdoors to take in the wonder of life and nature, to declare my divine right for perfect health, and to have intimate talks with God.

I am including here some of the specifics of my program. I give them to you not because I feel it is my place to suggest or prescribe treatment for any illness. Since I am not a doctor, I do not purport to offer medical advice or prescribe remedies for specific medical conditions. You must find and consult your own doctors and healers for that. I simply present my experience in an effort to expose you to some of the many options and resources available and, share what I feel works for me when I do it.

I think the best thing I did for myself overall was to follow a strict "macrobiotic" approach to eating for a period of six months. George Ohsawa, who turned to ancient Zen cooking methods in his search for personal health, first coined that term. Having cured himself of tuberculosis, he brought this wisdom to our Western world. His philosophy was that certain foods give life, and that in the skillful combining and balancing of foods, we are given the secret of life. *Macro* is derived from the Greek and means "great." *Bio* means "vitality," and *biotic*, the techniques of rejuvenation of life. Following this sound approach to eating, then, requires the selection and preparation of foods that produce longevity and cell rejuvenation.

I was first introduced to Macrobiotic eating years ago when we served as consultants to a group of natural food stores. As we and the owners became friends, Bill and I became acquainted with some unusual new foods. We discovered almost a craving for things like whole grain brown rice (considered to be the only "perfect" food) seasoned with tamari, a natural soy sauce, or even better, Bragg's Liquid Aminos. We developed an affinity for ramen noodles (not the grocery store kind loaded with MSG), miso soup, and even some seaweeds. We also began drinking a Japanese twig tea known as Bancha tea. It was as if some long unidentified bodily need was finally being met. Anytime Bill had a bout of painful bursitis (his father suffered from crippling arthritis), I fed him a stir fry of carrots, onions, broccoli, and sea vegetables, seasoned with tamari and served over brown rice, and the inflammation would disappear in one or two days. It's rather remarkable.

Now, years later, I was directed to *Recalled by Life*, a personal account by a physician who was cured of inoperable cancer by adhering to a strict macrobiotic diet. After reading it, I felt prompted to make the same commitment for myself. I had heard about a teacher and consultant on macrobiotic health through the East-West Center of Atlanta, and I contacted him for an appointment. His wife answered the phone, and after fifteen minutes of talking with her, I was convinced I could trust him to design a program for me.

During the consultation, I basically told him that I had an undiagnosed lump in my breast and wanted to cleanse, balance, and strengthen myself as much as possible before submitting to any medical intervention or treatment. He thought that was a sound approach. He then did a bit of testing and examined my hair, nails, eyes, and skin to determine how yin or yang (acid or alkaline) my body composition was. He explained that acid foods, yin (pronounced yeen), are high in potassium and they expand. For instance, sugar is yin; sugar, when placed on the tongue, tends to expand. Alkaline foods, yang (pronounced yahng), are high in sodium and they contract. Salt is yang; salt, when placed on the tongue, tends to contract. Whatever elements affect the mouth, he explained, invariably affect the body, which in turn affects the mind. This explains the profound effect that excessive or improper eating and drinking have on all aspects of our health.

Next, my consultant outlined the proper approach in food selection and preparation to bring about the desired balance and harmony in my body. The diet consisted mainly of whole grains and grain products, raw leafy vegetables, steamed round and root vegetables, beans and bean products, seeds, and nuts. I was to have two sea vegetables each day, as well as a particular type of sour pickle. He specified certain soups, seasonings, condiments, oils, and, for a sweetener, pure Vermont maple syrup. I could have an Irish potato no more than once a week, to be balanced by sea salt. He allowed a maximum of 4 to 6 ounces of seafood or fish per day, and surprised me with this caveat: he would rather I have a piece of Coleman beef (strictly corn-fed and natural) than any chicken. He explained that not only are most chickens force-fed large amounts of fillers and chemicals, they are confined in cramped quarters for easy feeding and fattening, and thus eat their own excrement in the process. He said I was to limit my alcohol intake to imported German beers made in accordance with strict German brewing codes, such as St. Pauli Girl or Beck's. He objected to almost all wine, with the possible exception of certain Japanese plum wines or sake, since most wines contain sulfites. He ended with other allowable beverages (purified water, bancha tea, fresh carrot juice), seasonal fruits, and natural snacks. He emphasized quality and variety over quantity, implying that I should eat about half as much as I normally would. He gave me some basic recipes and instructions for proper food preparation, and suggested macrobiotic cookbooks and cooking classes.

In addition, my consultant discussed other lifestyle guidelines. He emphasized the importance of getting large amounts of oxygen into my system through vigorous walking, yoga stretching, strengthening postures, even massage. He encouraged me to start *feeling* again, to start moving and expressing my emotions. This reminded me that I had once heard cancer referred to as "The Silent Scream." What was my body screaming to me, I wondered? What emotions did I harbor that were going unexpressed?

Before leaving that day, I arranged to return at a later date for a shiatsu massage. When I did return several months later, my general state of well-being (skin color and texture, flexibility of joints, etc.,) caused him to state, "If you have cancer, I'm a monkey's uncle!" I left feeling assured that I was making significant progress.

What may seem quite natural for others was, for me, the most difficult or extreme part of the macrobiotic approach: liquefying all food before swallowing. This demands the chewing of each bite a minimum of 30 to 50 times. This standard, referred to by Ghandi as "chew your drink, and drink your food," seemed both impossible and unrealistic. Like many Americans, I tend to be the eat-and-run type, more of a stuffer or gobbler than a chewer. The purpose behind this standard is to activate the enzymes required for the digestion and assimilation of the nutrients into the body. The other essential wisdom was to learn to stop eating before you are full. The only way to do this is to get up from the table while you are still a little hungry and to get used to feeling that way.

It is amazing how easy it is to make certain lifestyle changes when you think your life is being threatened, and how difficult it can be without that threat. If your life has not personally been touched in some way by a killer disease, it is easier to rock along, feeling removed from such a threat. Even my experiences as a hospice volunteer, supporting terminally ill cancer patients and their families, had become remote to me. (It is not a pleasant way to die.) Sometimes life needs to hit me over the head with a two-by-four in order to get my attention! Once refocused, however, I relentlessly pursued the dissolving of that mass and the achievement of optimal health.

I continued to read, developing a substantial library of resource books and materials. I read, for instance, about an herbal tea (known as essiac) first brewed by Native American Indians that has cured "thousands of patients with all kinds of cancer," according to Dr. Charles Brusch, personal physician to President John F. Kennedy. Elsewhere, Dr. Brusch stated that this was the remedy used to save President Kennedy's nephew, who lost a leg to what had previously been considered a fatal cancer. I also investigated Chinese herbs. Traditional Chinese medicine dates back several thousand years. It is based on the belief that the body's systems or organs, like the heart or kidneys, don't become ill on their own. They believe the environment you create in your body permits disease to "poke holes" in your immune system.

I also came across some amazing stories of both cancer and AIDS patients beating the odds and living years beyond their expectancy. Friends did research and sent me the latest medical opinions and updates.

I sought out other health experts and attended public seminars. One of the most informative was a meeting conducted by the American Institute for Cancer Research to present the bottom line on their collective knowledge to date. The main emphasis was that it is never too late to reduce cancer risk and that the major risk factors are in our control.

When asked if it wasn't just a matter of luck whether or not you get cancer, the emphatic response was, "No. In many cases you make your own good luck." Scientists now believe, they reported, that most cancers are caused by factors we can personally control; there are specific ways to reduce the chances of getting cancer. Although with regular exposure to carcinogens over the years, cancer risk rises, everything does not cause cancer. More than 80 percent of all cancers are associated with three lifestyle factors we can control: diet, smoking, and exposure to the sun.

What I learned, in brief:

Smoking—accounts for 30 percent of cancer deaths, and makes you more susceptible to other carcinogens, especially airborne pollutants. Stop the use of all tobacco products, and be aware that smokeless tobacco can cause cancer of the mouth.

Diet—40 percent of all cancers in men, and 60 percent of all cancers in women, are associated with diet; eating vegetables (broccoli, cauliflower, red and green peppers, carrots, sweet potatoes), fruits (citrus, cantaloupe, peaches, strawberries), and whole grain products supplies nutrients and other substances that may prevent cancer; too much dietary fat has been linked over and over with increased cancer risk (your very best choice is olive oil); low-fiber diets have been linked to colon and breast cancers; if you choose to drink coffee, water-processed decaffeinated is your best choice. Women should limit their intake of alcohol to no more than one drink daily, men to two; consume very little salt-cured, pickled, or smoked foods.

Sun—at least 50 percent of all melanomas, the most deadly form of skin cancer, and 90 percent of lip cancers are caused by overexposure to the sun; limit your exposure to the sun from 10 a.m. to 3 p.m., when it is the brightest, and always wear protective clothing and sunscreen of at least SPF 15.

I haven't "done sun" in 25 years, except for one trip to Cancun, Mexico, 15 years ago, where I made the mistake of deciding to "have something to show" for having been there. I did a one-day blitz in the sun using a low SPF suntan oil. What I had to show for my outrageous foolishness that night was an excruciatingly painful burn and no comfortable way to sleep or wear clothes. After I returned, a precancerous sore on my right thigh developed. When it failed to heal, I sought a dermatologist, who did an immediate biopsy. A few days later, he performed a procedure termed "burning it off." A similar place appeared on my left thigh a few years later, and I am now religious about protecting myself from the sun.

I had the privilege of meeting, and attending a workshop conducted by, Etel DeLoach, a woman with so much healing power in her hands that it has actually been photographed using Kirlian photography, and those pictures are on display at the Smithsonian Institute. Medical doctors who have run the course in their own skill or knowledge often consult her. Etel emphasized how easily stress can take its toll, and how important it was to make choices and re-sort priorities. She wanted me to adopt a philosophy of "me first." She thought carrot juice to be of value, particularly with the addition of the herb comfrey. She said to eat brown rice and fresh cooked beets every day. She emphasized how important attitude was in combating any illness. "You have to confront what your stress is," she said. "Meditate on your unique self and your life's contribution. Talk to God about this, and listen to what you're told."

I met with people who formerly had cancer and survived, including a man who had recovered from colon cancer. After cleansing away forty pounds and the colon tumor, he started his own business dedicated to putting others in touch with the products and resources that helped restore him to perfect health. He strongly suggested that we invest in a water purifier with a reverse osmosis membrane to filter all foreign substances from our kitchen tap water, and he recommended that I drink copious amounts of water daily. He also introduced us to the use of a little-known gadget called an Accuspark that could help clear whatever static was in my lymphatic system. He spoke of success with visualization processes, such as picturing the lump growing smaller and affirming that "it is going away." (I was already familiar with the innovative mind-body work done in the 1970s and outlined in Carl and Stephanie Simonton's book, *Getting Well Again*, and the remarkable results they were having in cancer control.)

As in my previous experience, this resource favored the use of herbal formulas that strengthen the immune system. He suggested I read the new research on the use of shark cartilage and investigate the use of blue-green algae. Following the principles of food combining, he said he ate only fresh fruit the first four hours of the day, followed by lots of carrot juice, and organic vegetables of mixed colors. He felt cabbage and spinach were particularity important. He said he used to suffer from chronic allergies and colds, but with the addition of high quality bee pollen to his diet, he had not had a cold in five years.

I was also introduced to another Atlanta entrepreneur whose personal story was quite amazing. After having been diagnosed with endometrial cancer, she conceived and gave birth to a "miracle baby," giving credit to a strict macrobiotic diet. My new friend provided a great deal of emotional support and introduced me to Atlanta grocery stores and restaurants that sell and serve natural foods.

Out of all this, I developed a five-part campaign: information gathering, increased physical activity, choosing foods that heal, reducing stress-producing factors, and devoting time to my nurture and total well-being.

My basic program included the following:
- Prayer and meditation
- Lots of oxygen through running/walking
- 8 to 16 oz. fresh carrot juice
- At least 8 glasses of purified water
- Personalized macrobiotic diet
- Use of the Accuspark
- Supplemental herbs to strengthen immune system
- Supplemental vitamin C and E
- Music therapy
- Visualization
- Breathing and stretching through yoga exercises
- Removal from high stress situations
- Gathering emotional support
- Using a "vent partner" for emotional release

- Massage
- Bill's "laying on of hands" to the crown of my head each morning, accompanied by loving, soothing words
- Ultra-sound galvanic and warm castor oil packs on the affected area
- A colonic flush to remove accumulated toxins
- Learning to say "no" more often

At the end of six months, I felt physically and emotionally strong and ready for a medical evaluation. I scheduled a mammogram and an appointment with my gynecologist (who would have preferred for me to come in after only one month of doing my own program) for a complete examination. Although the mammogram indicated a mass, it "didn't look threatening." He sent me to a specialist, who concurred but wanted to aspirate and biopsy some fluid in the area. The fluid was tested and looked "remarkably clean." Since then I have had regular check ups. There have been no irregularities in either breast.

The main message I want to convey to you is to take good care of yourself and those you love. It is within your power to do so. Even in adverse circumstances, you are not a victim of chance or fate. Remember that all effects have causes and that we can reap only what we sow—it's an ancient life principle. Like me, you are responsible for, or the cause in, your own life. And while they are in your care, you are responsible for your family.

During a CSTN teleconference, stress expert Esther Orioli stated, "The body always whispers before it shouts." I thank God that this is so. Please pay attention to yours and what it is saying.

Most of us entrepreneurs have encountered the unimaginable and have lived to share our experiences. With the passage of time, our worst stories become the ones we love to tell on ourselves—our favorite war stories. When asked by his wife how he could joke about certain aspects of the Civil War, Abraham Lincoln responded, "I laugh, Mary, because I must not cry."

The Power of Laughter

As we learn to lighten up and bring more humor into our lives, things take on a different perspective—we become enlightened. You have heard, I'm sure, why angels can fly: It's because they take themselves lightly! Laughter provides a different outlook, takes your attention from yourself, and helps you think clearly and decisively. It relaxes and heals as almost nothing else can. I recently heard a statistic to the effect that a typical four-year-old laughs several hundred times a day. Somewhere around the age of eight, however, our laughter starts getting us in trouble with the authority figures in our lives, and by the time we reach adulthood our laughter ratio is reduced to perhaps fifteen times a day at the most.

Comedian Dick Gregory tells the story of his early childhood in poverty, the struggle growing up, striving to "make it" in the white-dominated entertainment business, and the enormous pride of success when he finally did. As a symbol of his new affluence, he bought a mansion in a very exclusive Los Angeles neighborhood. A few days after moving in, as he was mowing his lawn, a neighbor who was out of town the day he moved in came over. "Hey boy," his neighbor asked, "what do you get for mowing this lawn?"

Without blanching, Gregory replied, "I get to sleep with the lady inside!"

So stay as loose as you can, and realize that the tough times, failures, and mistakes provide us with two great gifts: (1) they give us direct feedback, allowing us to correct and make changes, and (2) they hone our sense of humor, helping us to remain humble.

As John Glenn suited up for his historic 1962 space mission, a reporter asked him what would happen if the space capsule didn't successfully come back. Glenn's succinct reply: "It would spoil my day."

Chapter 10

Doing unto Others

It is not that people resist change. People actually desire change. What they resist is your attempt to change them.

—William J. Schwarz,
Mastering the Forces of Change

LIFE PRINCIPLE:

Do unto others as you would have it done unto you.

ONE OF THE GREATEST opportunities life offers us for personal and spiritual growth is in our relationships. Have you ever noticed that the minute you commit to yourself to stay emotionally calm or serenely purposeful, someone comes along and messes it all up? If it weren't for all those darn people in our lives, look how much easier and less complicated things would be! Why is it that, without fail, our personal relationships are the one arena where everything we've talked about so far gets tested to the hilt?

Not only do our personal relationships test us, but they also force us to examine our own thoughts and behavior by providing a constant mirror in which we can see our own reflection. One candid look around you will reveal that almost everyone in your life is there either to be served by you or to reveal to you something you need to see in yourself.

In the entrepreneurial world, your relationships are one of your most valuable assets. There may come a time when your relationships and your skill in building and sustaining them are the only things you have left. The relationships you develop and sustain within your family, organization, and vendor partnerships are essential to your very survival—more so than having the right office building, advertising, or sophisticated, high-tech equipment. Without a doubt, if your people desert you, your entrepreneurial dream will die.

Yums and Yuks

Human beings are judgment machines. The next time you are in a group of people anywhere—at work, while shopping, even at church—force yourself to notice all the automatic judgments you are making about the people around you. Some you will view as "special" in various ways; others you will see as "different." I call this the yum vs. yuk phenomenon. Notice how you view everyone around you according to the way they look, how they act, or what they say. Who in your eyes do you judge as acceptable or even "special"—safe, appealing, and trustworthy? (In other words, a lot like you?) Those are your "yums." Who do you consider "different" or untrustworthy— those you either dislike, resist, or resent? Those are your "yuks." Become pause-a-tive for a moment: Who do they remind you of? What do they trigger in you? Notice how you unconsciously go through this process with everyone you meet.

The corporate world is ruled by positionality. Yet any attempt to hold yourself as special, above, or "better" than someone else is always at the cost of the relationship and your peace of mind. What is different calls for a judgment, which must be made by someone "better." The pursuit of eliteness or specialness will always bring you separation and pain.

The Challenging Relationship

Almost everyone I know has one particularly difficult relationship that is a constant challenge. It may be a close family member, a daughter or a son. It may be a member of your staff or a client. It's that one that your mind keeps being drawn to—the one that drains so much of your energy. Perhaps you find yourself having silent, mental conversations with that person, trying to wield your authority or control over them. If so, I certainly can empathize.

Some years ago, someone came into my life who had the power to provoke me as no other could. This person absorbed an enormous amount of my thought and energy when I let her. Perhaps because we were so different in so many ways, I found it difficult to free myself of judgments about her and almost impossible to think of her with unconditional regard. No one triggered the response in me that she did. It ranged from anger to apathy. She was, however, a part of my extended family and a given in my life.

In time, I discovered both a context and a tool that enabled me to view her with a more accepting heart and loving eyes. Perhaps the following information will be helpful to you in your most challenging relationships.

The Context

My context is that all communication is either a call for help or an act of love. Equally, I have come to recognize that the people in my life who appear most difficult or irritating are actually serving me by providing a mirror in which I can see those aspects within myself that I dislike in them. They also provide a way for me to view my emotional and spiritual maturity. Out of this expanded context, I endeavored to look into the heart of this particular person, to have compassion for her, and even to see her through the eyes of Christ. My ideal was to be trigger-free and not to take personally anything she did. But above all it was to love and accept her unconditionally by looking through the outer appearance to the perfect Self within.

The Process Tool

Often, the things we resist or dislike in another person are the things we fear to see in ourselves. That is the wisdom of the American Indian saying to "Never judge a man until you have walked a mile in his moccasins." Ken Keys, Jr., in his *Handbook to Higher Consciousness*, provides us with a process that can serve as a consciousness-expanding tool and "Instant Love Doubler": "Expand your love, your consciousness, and your loving compassion by experiencing everything that everyone does or says as though you had done or said it."

This is such a powerful frame of reference! While we are usually aware of the inside reasons and feelings that account for what we do, when we perceive similar behavior in another person we usually interpret it differently than we do our own thoughts and actions. This, Keys says, leads to such psychological conjugations as,

I am firm, you are obstinate, he is pigheaded.

I am frank, you are blunt, she is rude.

I enjoy my food, you overeat, he is a glutton.

I occasionally correct people for their own good,

You are quite argumentative, she has a terrible temper.

Although the external actions in the above examples could have been the same, the thought process used to interpret the situations was entirely different.

The purpose of this method is for you to use the same programming to perceive and interpret the actions and words of other people that you use in understanding your own actions and words. This requires you once again to be pause-a-tive. Pause for a moment and delay your reactions to any person or situation long enough to run it through the same programming you reserve for yourself. You may find that your ability to understand and love other people will instantly double. When it does, your response will indubitably be like mine: "There, but for the grace of God, go I." By consciously experiencing what another person does or says, you begin to realize that you would probably say and do the same things if you were they. This is true empathy.

In the case of the person I mentioned above, it also helped me to pause and remember that we were given neither the same gifts nor the same life course. By using this tool, I began to realize that often, when I felt irritated or angry and alienated myself from her, she was doing exactly the same things I had done at one time—and which I had probably found a way to accept in myself at that time. Do I do thoughtless, self-centered things? Yes. Am I careless and break things? Of course. Do I eat and drink things that aren't good for my health? Sometimes. Do I seek ways to hide out when I don't feel safe? Sure I do. Do I say I am going to do things and then don't do them? On occasion. Have I taken things that don't belong to me? Regrettably, I have. The value-added benefit from this process is that I am striving to have unconditional love and acceptance for myself, as well. I am learning to forgive myself.

What Is Unforgiven Is Unforgotten

The lack of forgiveness is the most destructive, most debilitating force imaginable between individuals or nations. The failure or unwillingness to forgive each other or ourselves destroys physical, emotional, and spiritual health, divides families, and causes nations to go to war. In his book *Stay Alive All Your Life*, Dr. Norman Vincent Peale calls ill will "dislocated harmony," which results in sickness and dis-ease (disease). He quotes a New York physician who says that 70 percent of his patients reveal resentment in their case histories. "Ill will and grudges help to make people sick. Forgiveness will do more toward getting them well than any pill."

I recently witnessed the life-destroying power of unforgiveness in the life of someone dear to me. A longtime friend discovered she had breast cancer. As an intelligent and aggressively determined woman, she tackled her cancer with full force. The will to stay alive and see her adolescent daughter grow to womanhood was very strong. She researched and studied. She questioned and challenged. She medically fought her cancer in every way she knew: she underwent a radical mastectomy and chemotherapy, and later a bone marrow transplant. She also combined the best of traditional medicine with nutrition and herbs. The one thing she failed to do forgive.

Through the years I knew her, this woman carried anger and blame toward her father and mother, who also died of cancer, for an unhappy childhood. When her cancer was considered to be in remission, she became angry and bitter toward her best friend, who had attempted to share her own religious conversion and beliefs. Judging that her friend was being self-righteous, she abruptly cut off an intimate twenty-year relationship. She refused to forgive the perceived wrong—that her friend was trying to change her—and wouldn't let it go. In spite of all her friend's efforts to repair the relationship and make amends, she refused to take her phone calls, to answer or acknowledge her letters, or to let her back into her life. The last time I spoke to her when she was alive, the bitterness that came across the phone was toxic and resolute. I have no doubt that this is what actually killed her. Her spirit of love and forgiveness died first—and her body followed.

Give As Before

Who do you need to forgive? Forgiveness is fourfold:
- We forgive others for whatever we perceive them to have done to us (remembering that all perception is mis-perception).
- We forgive ourselves for having taken things personally and for the separation this has caused.
- We also forgive ourselves for any thoughtless thing we might have said or done which hurt another, and we ask them to forgive us in turn.

Without forgiveness, we cannot be emotionally free or spiritually blessed. Until goodwill flows from you, it cannot flow to you. Step out in faith, now, as you read this. Focus on your heart and simply say, "With God's help I now forgive_____." Dr. Peale has suggested repeating the Lord's prayer with these changes: "Forgive me my trespasses_____(insert)_____as I forgive_____" and inserting the offender's name. Dr. Peale continues, "Ask for a spiritual rebirth with all resentment tendencies removed." "Sincerely want this, pray for it, believe it is given you and you will have it," he affirms. What greater gift could we give ourselves than an untroubled mind?

The acid test that we have truly forgiven is that we suffer no guilt and we give as before. That's how we know forgiveness is accomplished. Although a memory may linger, there will be no sting.

What Is Your Operating Climate?

Any time we interact with someone out of our misjudgments, we cause that person to react and become protective. Instead of giving us feedback, the people around us tend either to "go away" mentally or physically or to fight back to preserve their own psychological safety. In this way, we are often not aware of the effect we have on others or the way others see us. Jack Gibb, a professor of Organizational Psychology, provided our Learning Laboratories students with a method of determining the type of climate we create around us as parents, managers, or salespeople.

Assesment Worksheet

As you look at the following 12 words, make a mental checklist. Which column best describes your way of operating around others?

Evaluation	Description
Control	Problem Orientation
Strategy	Spontaneity
Neutrality	Empathy
Superiority	Equality
Certainty	Provisionalism

Make a commitment to one column or another and check the appropriate word. Which set of terms best describes your personality or management style? Do you think of yourself as being strategic and a control specialist? Or do you see yourself as more spontaneous and empathetic?

If the left-hand column seems to best describe your interpersonal style, Jack Gibbs says this tends to build fear, defensiveness, and uncertainty on the part of the people with whom you are communicating. If the right-hand column describes your style, then you are building supportiveness. Your relationships are warmer and more trusting.

As we compare these words two at a time, try to think of synonyms and examples that you can remember from your own experiences. Consider how you honestly react to these illustrations.

Evaluation versus Description. To most managers and parents, evaluations are just basic judgments. But consider the role of a judge. Someone ends up right and someone ends up wrong. How do you react when you're being judged? One of the greatest barriers to communication is our tendency to judge from our point of view rather than trying to understand from another person's point of view.

Any attempt to change another person's feelings or to judge how someone ought to feel can only be met with defiance or withdrawal. If we are entitled to anything in life, it is to our feelings. I own my feelings. And you own yours, and you're entitled to express them. When our children were growing up, Bill and I encouraged them to express their feelings of anger with us. Listening to them describe how they felt about what we were doing (spending long hours with clients and students away from them) wasn't easy—it can sound very personal. But feelings are not right or wrong—good or bad—they're just feelings. To the extent they were allowed to express their upset or negative feelings, we knew they would equally be able to express their feelings of appreciation and love.

On college campuses today, students publish books that rate every professor. They even sell advertisements in them! Along with the professor's name and course title is an in-depth evaluation and rating system of the course and the teacher's effectiveness. The teacher used to evaluate the student, and now the student is evaluating the teacher. That's part of change. If it's viewed as a threat, we are going to react defensively. If it's an opportunity to improve and cope creatively with a situation, we are going to get better.

Control versus Problem Orientation. Anytime you attempt to change or control another person, you create a police state where you are not only the jailer but also the jailed. Remember—whatever you hold onto has a hold on you. How do you feel about someone who is trying to exert control over you? Do you feel trusting and able to disclose information? Or do you feel protective and resentful? Recall how you as a buyer felt when a salesperson was controlling the interview and trying to sell you something, versus being there to help you solve a problem. There is a world of difference. It is uncomfortable, perhaps impossible, for you to buy something when you are being "sold." On the other hand, it is difficult to resist or resent someone whose posture is, "I'm here to serve you."

Strategy versus Spontaneity. Some people always have a personal agenda. Even in a simple conversation, you can sense that hidden, unspoken force at play. How do you feel when someone has you in his or her master plan? You know you fit in somewhere, but you are not sure where. I find this very unsettling.

Entrepreneurs tend to have a strategy for everything—even taking vacations. In the early years of our marriage, my husband could not consider going on vacation without a desk full of work or a suitcase of books. It just wasn't in his comfort zone. Once he got into the vacation mode, however, he would become spontaneous and creative, and the books would lie unopened. As we learn to respond to things on a situational basis, we become more spontaneous. Now he is great fun on vacations! And in interpersonal relationships, he has developed an easy, relaxed way of being with people that once felt foreign to his "loner" personality.

Neutrality versus Empathy. Many people think the opposite of love is hate. I think it is apathy. Hate requires strong emotion and is actually the flip side of love. Apathy infers neutrality—a lack of emotion, caring, or commitment. It implies total indifference. Indifference is death, not only to ourselves but to all those around us.

Any time I take a neutral position—think something or someone doesn't concern me—life will directly see to it that it does!

Superiority versus Equality. There is a notable difference between positional superiority and personal superiority. People you deal with will accept positional superiority, meaning that you're my boss and that's the way it is on the organizational chart. They can accept the fact that positionally you are superior, but they won't accept personal superiority. The problem with positional superiority is that you tend to convey it with personal superiority. The resultant feelings are defense-producing and intolerable. Equality is so essential to personal growth and full humanness that we will do whatever it takes—even give our lives—to achieve it.

Certainty versus Provisionalism. One of the most difficult things for most parents, managers, and salespeople to understand is that certainty builds defensiveness. Certainty means that you have all the answers. If you have all the answers, then there is no room for anyone else.

I come from a line of highly opinionated women. As a teenager, I can recall riding with my mother in her compact sports car as she strongly expressed her views on political figures and issues. (Never mind that she was intuitively on-target about Nixon.) She spoke with such certitude and infallibility that I was unable to sort through or express my own opinions. I felt trapped and unable to breathe, desperately wanting to escape that barrage of "rightness."

Being provisional implies that your opinion or knowledge is adequate for the time being, or for the situation at hand, not that you alone have all the right answers.

Understanding Ourselves and Others

Through each of us there runs a deep, limitless river of emotional energy. Through years of childhood survival, this energy has moved into a protective comfort zone and become damned up into a rigid behavior style. This comfort zone can be observed as both a social style of predictable behavior and a survival backup style that we exhibit when we feel threatened in some way.

Any time you act to fulfill your needs by selling, telling, or controlling, the person you are dealing with must seek to fill theirs by going into a protective mode. This creates a deficit relationship and results in a duo-log—think of two TV sets talking to each other—rather than a dialogue. Then communication becomes sensing and reacting to what you are doing to them, rather than hearing and responding to what you are saying. They will see you as trying to change them or get something from them. They will feel no safety and will protect or defend what they see as theirs or seek autonomy. In a sales situation, for instance, this results in a no sale.

In any situation of perceived threat, the natural flow of emotional energy gets "backed up" into one of four defensive, nonnegotiable postures or behavior styles. These are characterized by either *fight* or *flight*. From observing this situation, Dr. David Merrill has pinpointed four specific, identifiable *back-up* styles that describe how people tend to react when they feel psychologically threatened. These ideas are invaluable in being able to see yourself clearly and to understand the behavior of others:

Analytical or thinking-oriented people adopt a *flight* mode and will avoid. "I'll think about it."	Driving or action-oriented people adopt a *fight* mode and will become autocratic. "No!" "Because I said so!"
Amiable or relationship-oriented people adopt a *flight* mode and will acquiesce. "Whatever you say."	Expressive or intuition-oriented people adopt a *fight* mode and will attack. "You no good, how could you?"

Each quadrant represents an observable social behavior/comfort zone (analytical, driving, amiable, and expressive) and the co-relating back-up style/react mode (avoiding, becoming autocratic, acquiescing, and attacking), which surfaces when one's perceived survival needs are not being met.

People will often stay in their react mode until they find someone who doesn't represent a threat to them by providing the appropriate release or safety valve. These are the guidelines that will enable you to be that person when others feel pushed into a corner:

Allow space for making their own decisions.	Value their time.
Look at things from their point of view.	Give them applause or recognition.

Versatility and Impact

When someone has shifted into their back-up style, and you are trying to interact with them, you will likely be required to shift out of your own comfort zone and move into theirs. One way you can establish an immediate rapport is to mirror a person's voice tone, volume, and tempo. You can also subtly match their posture, gestures, or facial expression to quickly establish a state in which the person is most responsive to you. Establishing rapport and providing for the needs of others as outlined above will enable you to increase your versatility and personal impact as a more effective parent, teacher, manager, sales person, or leader.

Awareness Worksheet

Determine what judgments you have about each of the above social styles and survival modes. Whom do you see as the "good guy" or "bad guy?" What mode seems most sensible or familiar to you? Which is the least acceptable? Who in your family or life represents each style?

Who would you like to make an agreement with (someone close to you) that, should either of you feel threatened and go into your survival mode, the other would strive to provide the necessary safety valve to restore productive, harmonious communications? What would that be like? By when will you seek that agreement?

Providing Emotional Support

At this point, you have the context of service, and the resources of vision, purpose, commitment, and an empowered model of reality to support you in your relationships. It is time now to stop and address the overlooked emotional needs of your family. By providing your full attention now, in a constructive way, you prevent someone from having to seek it in a destructive one.

Ever wonder why little children misbehave when you are reading, cooking, or on the computer or telephone? It's because they are lacking something they crave—your attention. They would rather you yell at them, or even hit them, than ignore them. And the older they get, the more creative or dangerous their methods become for seeking love and attention. The tragedy that results from the lack of nourishment and attention can be prevented by recognizing the inherent needs each of us have, and providing them to ourselves and those we love.

As a family breadwinner, it is common to convince ourselves that everything we produce (including the missed meals and events, the long hours away from home, the tension or stress) is for the direct benefit of the family—"After all, I'm only doing this for you!" Well, try telling this to your preteen daughter or your son after missing one more birthday, recital, or championship play-off.

Inc. magazine's Entrepreneur of the Year, Max Carey, will never forget the devastating confrontation with his teenage daughter, Elise, as he left for his umpteenth week out of town: "Don't tell me you work this hard for me," she chided, stopping him cold. "You do it for yourself. You'd do the same thing even if we weren't around." A few feeble rebuttals later, Max was forced to admit she was right.

"It's hard to acknowledge to my family how much I love the business," he confessed recently. "The truth is, it's my reason for being. I was hoping it sounded less selfish to say I was doing it for them."

It is unfortunate that the qualities that result in high achievement and success in business (risk-taking, high demand or control, and hardball or no-nonsense tactics) do not translate well into spousal or parental effectiveness. In fact, they often have the reverse effect—causing resentment, alienation, and destructive, attention-producing behaviors. Even worse, your attempts to directly change that behavior will only create further resistance and reinforce defensive, rigid patterns of behavior in yourself.

Although our family members may be as dear to us as life itself, the thrill of the chase and the desire to succeed will always block out their needs, if we let them. So how do you juggle personal ambition and escalating business demands with the emotional needs of your family members and work group?

First, you have to become physically and emotionally available to them. You have to show up and be accessible, not in a simply dutiful or a preoccupied way, but in a manner that demonstrates their value to you. (Don't forget that any tension you carry home with you will automatically be projected onto them!) We learned the hard way when our children were still young that before any relaxed family interaction took place, Bill had to shift his gears. This meant setting his running shoes out in the morning so they were the first things he saw when coming home. Once he put the shoes on and ran a bit before he came into the house, he was free of the cares of the day and was able to maintain balance and harmony at home.

The Skills of Intervention

The majority of the time when we show up in someone's life we represent change. This can occur just by going to the office or coming home at the end of the day. When someone thinks you are trying to change him or her, they automatically feel threatened. (This is almost always the case in a sales situation.) And I suspect each of us has at least one relationship where damage has already been done. It may be with your spouse, a child or other family member, or an employee. This situation calls for you to use the skills of an interventionist.

To intervene means to go into a place where distrust, fear, or resistance exists, based on a past experience with you or the story of another's experience with you, and release the energy that has been blocked or suppressed. This energy is needed to establish trust and bring about change. It is created by addressing and moving through internal, instinctive barriers of self-protection, defense, denial, and deflection. These reactions are ways our mind protects and defends us from being hurt, used, or sold by someone else. Until trust is established, it is pointless to try to move into task.

Describe and Disclose

For years I have been using a marvelous little tool for bringing about change in any upset relationship. The reason it is so effective is that it eliminates all judgments of another person's behavior while letting them in on the effects of that behavior. The process is to describe the offending situation or behavior without accusation, and to disclose the resulting consequences and the desired outcome. Then ask for feedback. As you begin the intervention, you must be very clear within yourself what your purposeful intent is for the relationship.

Conflict Resolution Worksheet

The Telling-the-truth Model

When you said_____(or did)_____I felt_____.
And the judgment I made was that

_____

_____.

As a result, I have been (how you have been feeling and behaving).
What I want now as the basis of our relationship is

_____.

What I commit to do is_____.
My purpose in doing so is to _____.
Would you please give me some feedback?

This powerful little model effectively separates feelings from thinking, releases judgments or barriers, and serves as the springboard for a committed relationship and a new plan of action. I realize it calls for some staging. It's okay to make a copy of the format so you can use it as a cheat sheet while you go through the process. Do stick with the structure—it works!

The Forces of Change

In bringing about change, both junior and senior forces are available for our use, but they are not one and the same. *Junior forces* are *getting* forces. The traditional, high-control approach to change through policies, strategies, force, or fear is an example of junior forces at work. Another example is the traditional sales approach of tell-sell-close. Junior forces result in destructive counterforces and attempts to beat the system. They build walls of distrust, fear, resentment, and separation. Under these conditions, attention and energy are sucked up, leaving little available for purposeful pursuits except when driven by high stress, tension, and pressures. Although fear isn't a motivator, it does get things done—while destroying the doer.

Senior forces are *giving* forces. They are central to all successful living. They simply require you to let others into you, rather than you trying to change them. By doing so, you provide a safe environment that allows them to change. When senior forces are utilized, even the most difficult circumstances can be magically transformed into increased energy, closeness, trust, commitment, and shared vision. In understanding and working with these senior forces, you will gain a greater ability to contribute to and partner with your children, spouse, clients, and employees.

The forces of change are already present in the universe. They are the basis for all lasting change throughout time. Everyone wants change, wants to have his or her life work. What they resist is being changed—by you or anyone else. The three natural forces that must be present to bring about change are safety, freedom, and attention. Let's consider these one at a time.

Safety, in the psychological sense, means freedom from the threat of danger or injury. It is based on the fear of loss—of time, respect, money, love, etc. Anytime you don't provide it, others will seek it.

Behaviors that destroy a sense of safety include being judgmental, not keeping your word, looking out for you own self-interests, and withholding information or affection. What we tend to think of as defensive behavior is the natural tendency to seek safety from being changed, sold, or controlled.

Freedom implies the liberty to be unconstrained by a given person, condition, or circumstance. All rebellion is an effort to be autonomous and free from imposed restraints. When we impose our will on others, the only freedom we leave them is to do the opposite. Responsible behavior can only be present where freedom exists.

Attention is observant consideration or thoughtful notice. Whatever we give attention to, grows stronger in our lives. Whatever we take attention away from, withers and dies. Attention-seeking behaviors can include the accumulation of material things or status symbols, obsession with getting ahead, or being #1. When attention is not provided, people tend to rebel or withdraw, resulting in destructiveness, emptiness, loneliness, depression, hypertension, and over- or under-achievement.

All of these elements—safety, freedom, and attention—must be present for trust to exist. Although trust is often discussed in salesmanship, leadership, and parenting training, how to build trust and a true partnership is seldom understood. The senior forces must be present for any lasting change to take place.

Awareness Worksheet

Awareness Exercise for Providing Safety:

1) Who seeks safety when they are around you?
How is this demonstrated in their behavior?
2) Who currently isn't around you because you are not safe?
What have you done to take that safety away?
What lack has this created in your life?

Awareness Exercise for Providing Freedom:

1) What happens when you want someone to do things your way?
How are they then free to behave?
2) What does trying to control others turn you into?
Who ends up being controlled?
Who in your life is demonstrating freedom-seeking behaviors?
How?

Awareness Exercise for Providing Attention:

1) Who currently isn't safe, free and alive through your lack of total attention?
What are their attention-seeking behaviors?
2) When someone tries to get your attention, what freedom do you have?
What judgments do you make?
How safe do you feel with them?
How safe are they with you?

The discovery of senior forces has been the source of all lasting change throughout time. These three forces—safety, freedom, and attention—combine to provide the autonomy the human spirit will fight and even die for. They are as essential to change as breathing clean air and drinking pure water is to maintaining health and life itself. As you utilize the senior forces of change, you release the energy required for trust, cooperation, and growth. As you provide safety, freedom, and attention to those around you, they are better able to support you in your dream, and you provide what they need in order to have theirs.

Chapter 11

Trusting in God

... when life knocks you to your knees—well that's the best position in which to pray, isn't it? On your knees. That's where I learned.

> —Ethel Barrymore, beloved
> actress of stage and screen

I believe we are free, within limits, and yet there is an unseen hand, a guiding angel, that somehow, like a submerged propeller, drives us on.

> —Rabindranath Tagor, Indian philosopher, poet, and Nobel Prize winner

Without the Father, I am nothing.

> —Jesus of Nazareth

LIFE PRINCIPLE:

The kingdom of God is within you.

TRUE VISION IS BORN OF THE SPIRIT. It requires a venturesome faith to step out into the unknown and act as if what you envision is already so. The only way you can embrace the unknown is through trust: trust in yourself as the creator of your life experience, and trust in your Heavenly Creator, who set up the system to work perfectly and to support you fully. The ability to trust is one of the key issues of life. We only develop trust or become trustworthy *by trusting.* Unless we trust in Life by trusting ourselves and our own guidance system, then doubts, fear, greed, and the constant need for outside confirmation will prevail.

On the surface, it may appear to you that the entrepreneurial life is a rather worldly life driven by the competitive, egotistic pursuit of material things. But in reality, as you will see, it can offer the opportunity for an incredibly spiritual life.

On January 27, 1989, I awoke around 3 a.m. in the grip of terror, my entire body covered in a cold sweat. Tightness engulfed my chest, and I could barely breathe. It took me a moment to clear my frantic mind, and then I remembered what was wrong. We had made the choice to decline an investment offer of $1 million, despite the fact that we had absolutely no money and no known available resources left.

This offer had represented our financial salvation by providing the funds we so desperately needed. But because of the multiple strings the investment group had attached to the contract, we decided to reconsider—even as the celebration champagne chilled in the refrigerator.

Emotionally exhausted, I forced my mind back to the present. I turned my head to discover my husband lying beside me, eyes wide open, staring at the ceiling, his body stiffened with fright.

What could we have been thinking? How could we have knowingly placed the future of our loved ones in danger, with even the slightest possibility of financial ruin, much less this virtual certainty of ruin? Who on earth could we turn to now? How would we get by, even for the next few days?

As the enormity of the situation hit both of us full force, Bill took me in his arms. Feeling completely vulnerable and fully humbled, my husband and I clung tightly to each other. A soft whisper broke the thick silence. "Let's pray," he said

During the 17 years we had been married, except at mealtime, we had always prayed separately. This was the first time we actually got down on our knees together and prayed as one. We knew we had nowhere else to go and nothing left but our faith in God and the desire to live by His will. As we sought guidance and acknowledged our own powerlessness in the situation, our fear gradually subsided and a gentle peace settled over us. Without knowing how it would happen, our hearts were reassured that God would continue to sustain us, and we felt permeated with and united by His truly amazing grace.

In those precious moments, we found the strength to let go of our fear and allowed ourselves to be healed of the enormous toll that the accumulated stress had taken on our marriage. Praying together renewed our love, enabling us to simply live moment to moment, and day by day, in complete faith.

The very next day we were given 30 days to move from our new company headquarters, because the investor whose offer we had declined was also the owner of the building in which we had our offices. We had absolutely no idea where we could go. What we needed was a financial "angel," maybe even a miracle.

One month later, having developed a new and synergistic partnership, the nucleus of our company relocated to picturesque Winter Park, Florida. And although we would not have qualified to rent even a simple two-bedroom apartment, we miraculously found and were able to lease a lovely estate home with a separate guest house on peaceful Lake Mizel. This provided us with the means for housing and entertaining the stream of dignitaries, potential business affiliates, and clients who came to do business with us over the next six months.

It is my heartfelt belief and experience that life will always present you with the people and circumstances to facilitate your next stage of contribution or growth. A thoughtful look will quite likely reveal the times when coincidences, chance meetings, or unplanned circumstances provided a turning point in your own life. Most of us can even recall a time when, miraculously, our lives have been protected or spared. As you begin to acknowledge and honor those events that are not of your own making, your faith will continue to grow. And you will attune yourself to expecting, attracting, and experiencing miracles in your everyday life. The following incident illustrates how God provided for us even in the midst of the personal tragedy of our new partners, Esther and Jon Phelps.

One day, after we had been in Winter Park about a month, Esther called to say that there had been a sudden death in Jon's family, and they had to go out of town. She was wondering if their son Davey, a new friend of our son, Kord, could come and stay with us. Offering my condolences, I said, "Of course he can come," and we arranged for them to bring him by.

When the Phelps arrived, they came into the kitchen bearing sacks full of food! Esther explained that she had just shopped for groceries before they received the tragic phone call, knew the things wouldn't stay fresh, and hoped we could use some extra food. She also gave me $40 to cover Davey's entertainment or miscellaneous expenses.

What she didn't know was that we had no way to buy groceries during that time except at an Amoco Food Mart with our one remaining credit card. Or that I already had one house guest, Don Kremer, a potential business affiliate from Carmel, California, and was expecting two more.

The next day our affiliate John Roberts arrived from Phoenix, joined by a potential client from Atlantic Bell. I had not known what or how I was going to feed them. Esther's bountiful supply exactly matched my needs! I can still remember what I served at each meal. It was memorable to me because it was so perfect.

I don't remember what I required a day or so later, but that was handled by a small portion of "Davey's funds." I do remember my amazement and gratitude that they were available! Who says miracles don't happen?

The possibility of actually making our dreams real—of having it all—can, at some level or another, be frightening. Some of us suffer from the fear of failure; others from the fear of success. We forget that we were created for winning, not losing. Being effective and successful often goes against our long-held beliefs about ourselves or the way life is. We're so used to compromise, substitution, or just getting by. Or we possess the attitude of my teenage years, "Oh well—I didn't want that anyway." We have difficulty trusting God to actively supply our heart's desire. We are not sure we are either deserving or trustworthy.

Carl Jung addressed this dilemma when he stated, "People become neurotic when they content themselves with inadequate or wrong answers to the questions of life. They seek position, marriage, reputation, outward success or money, and remain unhappy and neurotic even when they have attained what they were seeking. Such people are usually confined within too narrow a spiritual horizon."

Please trust that you have never had to—and never will have to—go it alone. And know that however powerful or successful you become, power comes (and always has) through you, and not from you. Make a conscious effort to be open to the stream of God's power and love. Let it in. Believe that you are worthy. Acknowledge God's goodness in your life. Trust that He seeks and desires with all His heart to have a vivid, personal relationship with you. That's part of our purpose in being here—to return to Him, through a loving, trusting spirit.

That which supports you and your vision will present itself at every stage of your life. God uses both the stepping stones and the stopping points in our lives to bring us closer to Him. He often works most clearly during the most difficult times. The tough part is recognizing and letting it in.

Finding Strength from Within

We practice being in the presence of God by venturing inward. Through the avenues of prayer and meditation, we glimpse the horizon of our divine potential. Both are exercises in discipline and solitude. Each requires time to be alone with yourself, an open and trusting heart, and the willingness to express to God your soul's sincere desire. Then still your mind, and listen for His response.

When we pray, we talk with God. When we meditate, we allow God to communicate with us. This practice begin each day with a personal experience of His presence. It adds dimension and scope to our lives, changing our perspective and reviving our spirit. It renews our dreams and highest aspirations, and enables us to rise above discouragement, defeat, or failure. It gives us courage and wisdom by clarifying once again our values and purpose. It lights the wicks of our spiritual candles, restoring us for our life's work and for daily life. It cleanses our minds of fear, guilt, and greed, and allows God to fill the vacuum with His goodness.

Prayer is:

- affirming our desire to realign our lives with the principles and will of God
- confessing our inability to consistently do that on our own.
- counting our many blessings regardless of appearances or circumstances
- validating the truth of God's guidance and grace
- enlisting and unleashing powerful angelic forces to come to our aid
- giving thanks for the opportunity to serve, and the power to grow personally and spiritually
- "making the heart large enough until it can contain God's gift of Himself"   —Sister Teresa, from *A Simple Path*

Always give as much of yourself as you can to as much of God as you understand. Even if you must, as Horace Bushnell once said, "Pray to the dim God, confessing the dimness for honesty's sake." Try saying to Him whatever you feel about Him. If you're not sure He exists, confess your doubts. If you feel He has let you down, tell Him so. Be willing to ask the tough, bitter questions from your heart: "How can I believe in You?" "Where were you when I needed You?" Let Him into your heart and mind, much as you did in the "describe and disclose" technique (in Chapter 10) with your family member or business associate. He can take it. He can handle it. He won't judge, retaliate, or condemn you because He is Love. So say it all—everything that stands in your way.

Then, when you are through telling—stop and listen. In the silence of the heart, God speaks. Give Him the opportunity to speak to you. God's interest in us is steadfast and trustworthy. Given any sort of a chance, He'll get through to you. Let Him love you back. And when you pause to listen, try to really hear the message for your heart. And then—here's the hard part—believe what you are hearing. Believe you are that significant, that worthy, that honored by

God to receive His blessing and guidance. And without asking "How?" quickly step forth to put that guidance into action.

Misperceptions of Meditation

Before I talk about what meditation is, perhaps I should say a few words about what it isn't. I am amazed by the misunderstandings in our Western culture, particularly in the Christian community, of the role of meditation in the spiritual life.

To begin with, meditation is not based on the occult, "New Age" practices, or the paranormal. It is a devotional act of deep reflection on sacred matters. The spiritually strongest and wisest people in history, including Jesus, King David, and the Buddha, were avid meditators—as was the great saint of our day, Mother Teresa.

According to the renowned Christian teacher Oswald Chambers, the meaning of the word meditation is "my heart consulted in me." "Meditation," he relates, "is an intense spiritual activity. It means bringing every bit of the mind into harness and concentrating its powers; it includes both deliberation and reflection." Elsewhere, he states, "Meditation means getting to the middle of a thing. It's how we can 'go in' to 'get out' of the muddle of things!"

Secondly, meditation does not mean simply making your mind a blank. Nor can meditation be equated with self-hypnosis or a state of acute suggestibility. In fact, the latter more accurately describes the normal waking state of the majority of people, as the hypnotists and wizards of Madison Avenue well know. Many of us are easily charmed and ensnared by the bombardment of advertising and other messages we see and hear each day. And for most of us, past conditioning and reactive behavior flow through our lives like a powerful river. Meditation actually de-hypnotizes, freeing us from the spell of daily deceit and illusion.

In our demanding external world, we are more typically oriented to feeling depleted, rather than being rejuvenated. Meditation opens us to an abundance of energy not otherwise available by tapping us into an internal wellspring whose fullness is not depletable. Even in today's advanced scientific arenas, meditation is being validated as having a remarkable effect on antiaging and stress reduction. Through its practice, the challenging activities we engage in on a daily basis can be organized from a different perspective, such that they are a part of our lives but not the whole of our lives. We experience the harnessing and focusing of greater compassion for the present, greater tolerance for our past, new insight into the future, and a greater sense of peace and stability about who we are and the events of our lives.

Meditation is

- a dynamic activity of our intelligence, love, will, and talent
- the practice of deeply rooting into our consciousness the words that embody our greatest needs for guidance or our highest ideals
- listening for inspiration with an intuitive ear
- discovering the presence of spirit (God) within our hearts and minds
- being receptive to the inflow of God's peace to heal and purify the hurts of the past
- realizing our oneness with all of Life
- allowing the Holy Spirit to illumine our minds with the answers we seek
- sinking into the deep well of God's eternal wisdom to develop our inner capacity for courage, generosity, wisdom, joy, patience, reverence, excellence, harmony, integrity, tolerance, wholeness, and the ability to care

There are many approaches or techniques for meditation. For more detailed guidance, I recommend Eknath Easwaran's excellent book, *Meditation—A Simple 8-Point Program for Translating Spiritual Ideals into Daily Life*. However, the following basic guidelines I have developed for myself over the years will get you well on your way to creating a center of quiet and stillness within yourself.

When and Where to Meditate

The best time to meditate is any fifteen to thirty-minute period when you can be alone and quiet on a daily basis. The same time of day should be routinely set aside until the habit of silence is established. If possible, choose a time when your stomach is not full (unless the only thing you will be able to focus on is food).

My favorite time is early morning, though I am not a morning person. It is always dark, it is often cold, and my mind seeks to lure me deeper into our warm featherbed. When the alarm goes off, those others of you who are not early risers must not stop to think about it. Just leap out of bed—even if you can't remember why you are getting up. Some people need to do a few simple exercises or yoga stretches to help their body catch up before going into their meditation area. I like to time my period of study, prayer, and meditation so it concludes at sunrise. The dawn symbolizes freshness and renewal, and reminds me of the miracle of God's creation. It's a marvelous way to start the day!

The place where you meditate is very important. If at all possible, set aside a room or quiet space in your home that can be used for nothing else. This area should be uncluttered and simply decorated. It will soon begin to have a strong spiritual association for you. The unconscious mind adjusts more easily when it accepts the suggestion that it is in a certain place, at a certain time, for a specific purpose. Gradually, your room or corner may become holy for you.

How to Begin

The correct posture for meditation is to sit erect (in a straight-backed chair; initially, it is preferable for it to have arms), head tilted slightly forward, feet flat on the floor. (If you can be truly comfortable, you may prefer to sit cross-legged on a floor cushion.) By rocking back and forth a bit, you can locate your "sit bones" and center yourself over them. Place your hands in your lap in any position you find comfortable. Wear comfortable, loose-fitting clothing.

Begin by noticing the movement of your breath. Breathing through both nostrils, count the number of units required for a full

201

incoming breath. After a brief pause, then allow the same count for your outgoing breath. Breathing from your diaphragm, let your belly push out with your incoming breath, as if you were filling a balloon with air. Then let your chest with its "balloon," and your shoulders rise in the same manner. Hold yourself motionless for an instant or two before letting the breath start to leave, collapsing your shoulders and chest first. The idea here is to develop focused awareness—you can do that by using a very easy, gentle breath. When you feel your breathing to be even, let your eyelids slide gently downward, allowing your awareness to slowly move into the area of your heart. If you are among those who fall asleep the minute they close their eyes, you may choose to keep them partly open and focused on an object, such as a lighted candle, in front of you.

What to Meditate Upon

Your meditation consists of the slow recitation of a favorite passage of scripture, such as the Twenty-third Psalm. Once it is memorized, stay with the same daily passage. Go through it word by word, proceeding very, very slowly. Concentrate on each word. It's fine to cluster a small helper word with one of substance, like this:

"The Lord....is....my....shepherd....I....shall....not...want."

Let each word drop slowly inward, one at a time. Why so slowly?

As one modern mystic has explained,

> *A mind that is fast is sick.*
> *A mind that is slow is sound.*
> *A mind that is still is divine.*

It is not easy to still your mind. The sickness of hurry and worry pervades our society, and most particularly, the world of business. It is particularly difficult to disconnect the senses, leaving the world of sight, sound, and random thought behind. The mind is an amazing trickster, and it will go to great lengths to invade your sovereign state. It has been running things for a long time, thinking that its main job is to manage your survival. Well, you have survived! Now it's time to move from survival to the development and expression of your higher self, and your mind won't give up easily. When it is necessary, I simply say, "Mind, you can rest now." Other experienced meditators suggest giving your mind specific rules the very first day, such as, "Any time you wander from the passage, you'll have to start over again."

As you go through your passage, resist any association of ideas. Let's say you are going along just fine until you reach the word *shepherd*. Shepherd reminds you of sheep—perhaps like the ones you saw in the movie *Babe*. An image of all those talking animals flashes into your mind, and it then asks, "Should you become a vegetarian?" And off you go! So keep to the words.

The selection of a scriptural passage for meditation has several purposes. One, it provides training in concentration. When we persist in fully concentrating on the passage, our mind becomes one-pointed and learns to obey us. Then we are no longer victims of a reactive state. We become capable of sustained endeavor. We learn the value of doing only one thing at a time.

Secondly, a passage that inspires us turns our attention to the spiritual ideals we wish to emulate. I have stated previously that what we give our attention to is what we become. People today are insecure because they persist in thinking about and going after things that have no capacity to give them security. By putting our full attention on such ideals, we cause them to become imprinted on our consciousness.

What to Expect Along the Way

In the beginning, it will seem impossible to avoid certain sensations in the body. You may find yourself rocking back and forth. If you experience drowsiness, draw yourself up; stay away from the arm of your chair or your back support. It is normal to experience any or all of the following reactions: Your body will likely resist. Your chair or position will be uncomfortable. There may be pressure or irritation of the skin, or an uncontrollable desire to move some part of your body. You may itch. A deep thirst may develop.

Do not pamper these distractions nor feel any guilt for being aware of them. We become so accustomed to taking a self-indulgent, instant-gratification approach to life that we have great difficulty denying ourselves every possible comfort. Breathing into the irritating or distracting area and staying focused on your passage or affirmation can achieve both discipline and self-mastery. Do this as often as necessary. Like most of life's irritants, "This, too, will pass."

As you progress and the desperate whirring of your mind slows down, a new set of images will begin to flood your consciousness from the unconscious. There may be lights, colors, faces, designs, pictures, or scenes, much like an interesting television show. It will be tempting to stop and look at these pictures or follow the action of these scenes and to consider this to be meditation. Don't give in. This isn't it. As with the attention on the body or the activity of the conscious mind, it is necessary to refocus awareness by moving your attention gently but firmly back to the passage or affirmation. The meaning of the words should be re-examined by holding them up and grasping them lightly. This allows you to retain focus on the words and their meaning.

During meditation, strong emotions may be activated. You needn't be hijacked by them. Just give them short labels such as "angry feeling," "remembering," or "sad feelings," and set them aside. They will gradually decrease, and more important, you will begin to identify yourself as an outside observer and not the person who is disturbed by these thoughts and feelings. Waves of positive emotion can also sweep over you. Sometimes I'm filled with wonder, or moved to tears. To continue concentrating on the affirmation even during waves of emotion can immeasurably deepen your meditation. This is a process of releasing through focused concentration.

One caveat: Professor Easwaran has likened entering into deeper consciousness to the process of descending into a cave. Like the rope that is used by a spelunker as he threads his way downward, the scriptural passage is the lifeline to be used by you, the meditator. Keep tightly gripped to your passage. It will guide you through all situations.

If breaking through the surface level of consciousness to a deeper level is ever frightening to you, open your eyes for a minute or two and repeat the passage in your mind. Then close your eyes again, focusing on the spot directly behind your eyelids, and resume your meditation. If the fear returns, repeat the process. You may want to offer a simple prayer of protection and guidance.

In the initial stages of your meditation, it is a good idea to focus on the same passage over and over. But in time, the words may lose some of their meaning, and it's wise to select a new passage. My personal favorite is the prayer of the gentle friar who exemplified a Christ-like transformation in his conduct, character, and consciousness, known as Saint Francis of Assisi. His words have an almost universal appeal. The prayer goes like this:

> *Lord; make me an instrument of thy peace.*
> *Where there is hatred, let me sow love;*
> *Where there is injury, pardon;*
> *Where there is doubt, faith;*
> *Where there is despair, hope;*
> *Where there is darkness, light;*
> *Where there is sadness, joy.*
> *O divine Master, grant that I may not so much seek*
> *To be consoled as to console,*
> *To be understood as to understand,*
> *To be loved, as to love;*
> *For it is in giving that we receive;*
> *It is in pardoning that we are pardoned;*
> *It is in dying to self that we are born to eternal life.*

As you advance in your meditation and reach the point of stillness, you may experience a great light. With it will come an enhanced and personal understanding of the words of the psalmist, "Be still, and know that I am God." It is at this point that your consciousness can be moved into the light, and a spontaneous awareness or knowing (perhaps in actual words) may occur. This experience is very personal and difficult to describe, as the meaning differs for everyone.

Many years ago, at a time when I was struggling with issues of unworthiness and self-forgiveness, I had an amazing experience that I would term a reunion with the Light. It was like a beautiful home-coming, with great rejoicing and celebration. I was able to view myself as a shining being among many other shining beings, and I knew this to be a reflection of our true divine nature. Years later, in my counsel-ing practice, this experience allowed me to hold this vision for my clients while they struggled through whatever guilt or destructive image they had made for themselves and to come out to the other side.

There is only one failure in meditation, and that is to fail to med-itate faithfully. A few minutes of concentrated meditation each day is far better than an attempt at longer periods of undirected day-dreaming. At the end of the fifteen to thirty-minute period, complete your recitation and gently bring your focus to the floor in front of you. You might want to test your feet and legs to make sure they haven't fallen asleep before standing up. As you go quietly about your day's activities, let your passage become the pattern and ideal for your interaction with others. For instance, I often find myself humming one of the hymn versions of the *23rd Psalm* throughout the day.

With persistence and patience, you will find that deep reserves of energy, better clarity of judgment, and an expanded sense of purpose soon appear. We become more intuitive and discerning, and the boundaries that seem to separate us from the rest of the world disap-pear. This is followed by a greater sense of love, joy, connectedness, and finally, "the peace that passeth understanding."

Meditation requires that we make our body a good ally. We become reminded that "the body is the temple" and we must give it what it needs for health and strength. Without a balance between meditation and physical activity, the temple deteriorates, and the mind tends toward irritability or acute restlessness.

In the outside world, we are bombarded by media onslaughts that report violence of every sort. When we stimulate the senses unduly, vitality flows out, leaving us drained physically, emotionally, and spiritually. As we exercise selective control over what we listen to, what we watch, what we read, we train the senses to conserve vital energy. No matter what happens outwardly in our lives, we are in no way defeated or dependent. It is then that we can give freely to others and courageously fulfill our life's purpose.

No Trouble Too Great

I was greatly surprised to find that it was easier for me to keep my focus on God during the difficult survival years than when things were going well. When times were the toughest, my faith was the strongest. It was impossible for our family to get through any single day without acknowledging our dependency and gratitude for God's intervention and guidance. But as things got better, my daily dependence decreased, and I became complacent and more self-dependent. I was turning God into my crisis counselor rather than my everyday companion.

Peter Grant, pastor of Atlanta's Buckhead Community Church, uses a wonderful analogy to illustrate this point. He tells how he teaches his children to swim by going into the water with them and holding them up with his hand under them for support. Then, as he walks back and forth in the shallow end of the pool, the children happily practice kicking their feet and mastering the various strokes. As long as they are in the shallow water, Peter relates, they are perfectly confident that they are safe, and that Peter will not let them drown.

One day, however, when Peter moved into deeper water, his son Colin started to panic. Terrified, he began to flail around, losing his concentration, and grabbing his dad for support. Peter tried to communicate, "Colin, it doesn't matter how deep the water is—you can count on me to not let go of you, no matter what."

Peter knows that whatever the depth is in the pool, it is only his hand that keeps Colin afloat. Likewise, in the situations of life, God doesn't know shallow from deep. As Peter says, God is saying to each of us, "There is no water too deep for Me. Take your eyes off the circumstances, and rely on Me."

President Abraham Lincoln carried one of the greatest burdens to ever befall a leader of men. In his wisdom and humility, he recognized that the weight of his responsibilities as a leader of a country torn apart by civil war was more than he alone could bear:

> *I have been driven many times upon my knees by the overwhelming conviction that I had nowhere else to go. My own wisdom and that of all about me seemed insufficient for that day.*

> —Abraham Lincoln

Reaching Out

As we learn to rely on God and experience His abundant blessings, our stewardship response should be to reach out and touch the lives of others. As Henri Beyle noted, "One can acquire everything in solitude—except character."

Shortly after her graduation from college, my daughter, Vail, and I heard about an opportunity for a day (we thought!) of service through AIDS Atlanta. After the volunteer coordinator explained to our group what AIDS was and wasn't—that it could only be contracted by exchanging bodily fluids, and that if we didn't plan to do that, we were in no personal danger—he read a list of the people to be served, and a description of their needs. Vail and I both felt a desire to visit the one woman on the list. We were given her name, address, and the directions to her apartment. We were also armed with Christian literature "in case the opportunity or need arose," and off we went, a bit uncertain what to expect.

As we approached, I recognized the name of the apartment complex. I had read about it in the local paper. It had disintegrated to such a terrible state of neglect and disrepair that the tenants had refused to pay their rent and sought governmental intervention. It was a heart-wrenching sight.

We were greeted at the door by a friendly, eccentric-looking woman and a beautiful preteen girl, the sister and niece of the woman we came to help. Behind them, seated in a wheelchair, was our charge for the day, a lovely slender woman I'll call Wanda. We also met her two sons, who proved to be extremely intelligent, obedient, and loving boys.

While I was trying to determine their needs, Vail was having a conversation with the oldest son, Duane. "How much are you folks getting paid to come here?" he asked.

"We're not getting paid anything," she replied.

"Then why are you here?" he asked.

"Well," she replied, "sometimes people need help."

"I don't need any help," he replied.

"Well," Vail said, "right now your mamma needs some help. And someday, Duane, you may need someone to help you."

Looking her straight in the eye, this seven-year-old boy retorted, "When I need help, I just look to the Lord!"

And so, we discovered, does his mother. (So much for the Christian literature!) Although her muscles were disintegrating from the disease she innocently contracted from her husband, Wanda's serene attitude of "This is my life, and I'll trust God to help me move through it each day" inspired us to become official, long-term supporters to the entire family, rather than helpers for a day

It takes courage to face illness or other potentially devastating conditions with equanimity and grace. It requires great fortitude to withstand the uncertainty of material loss. If you are suffering from this type of pain, please remember that material losses are things of the earth, of things that pass away, not of things that have eternal significance. As we practice the principles that lead to the mastery of ego and an expression of our higher self, we begin to experience those things that cannot pass away. We have a direct and intimate experience of divine love, wisdom, will, joy, and peace. And we treat each other with compassion and respect.

"The great use of life," wrote the American philosopher William James, "is to spend it on something that will outlast it." Allow God to work through you. When you are willing to listen for His voice, it will come in unexpected ways. That is how the idea for this book was born. Out of my sustained, surrendered state of dependency on His strength and guidance, I would awake in the early morning hours with strong impressions and chapter titles running through my mind. (At the time, I didn't realize that's what they were.)

In spite of all the exhilarating highs and devastating lows of almost 30 years of entrepreneurial living, it never occurred to me to keep a diary or journal to record these experiences. But once the internal commitment was made to follow this prompting and I sat down to write, the lessons of these years flowed effortlessly to me. All delays in the completion of this book have come from my choice to make other things a priority. Not once have I experienced a writer's block. It is now my habit to keep a book of blank pages by my bedside to capture any prompting or clarifications that come in those early, quiet hours. When we are striving to express our highest and best, we are expressing God.

How do you know when you are letting God into your life? By the zest and passion that you naturally generate when your heart and soul are purposefully committed to a great work. Not just in the good times—but especially in the dark and troubled and uncertain times. Then you know you are not just making a living, but you are fully living. Out of this surrender and joyful embrace of all aspects of life will flow a oneness in your relationship to yourself, to your family, to God, and to all of life.

Chapter 12

Correcting, Completing— and Celebrating!

A ship should not ride on a single anchor, or life on a single hope.

—Epictetus,
Greek philosopher

Energy doesn't die; it simply changes forms.

—Linda Vephula, Founder and
publisher, *Angel Times* magazine

> **LIFE PRINCIPLE:**
>
> *Energy can neither be created nor destroyed.*

THE ABILITY TO EMBRACE THE unknown requires the awareness that success in life is a journey—a process of change and renewal. I am not sure any of us ever fully "arrives."

In the process we began by pursuing the dream called Corporate Satellite Television Network, my husband, Bill, and I came to understand three final principles that are essential to successful entrepreneurial living: correction, completion, and celebration.

In Chapter 1, I emphasized the importance of staying focused on the big picture. There is one caveat in this regard: You can stay so focused that you lose the ability to see or hear the feedback around you.

Correction Requires Feedback

On one level, correction is a very simple concept. On another level, it is a very powerful principle that applies to all that seek to achieve their dreams.

The U.S. space program, NASA, provides us with one of the best models of this correction process. What do you recall about the United States' first trip to the moon? You know, of course, that our astronauts got there and came back safely. It was a heroic and historic first. But did you know that their craft was heading to the moon only about 8 percent of the time? The rest of the time was spent in a constant state of feedback and correction.

Feedback allows you to know both where you are and where you will end up according to the direction you are going. Like the creative process, it requires a willingness to ask yourself, "Where do I want to be, and what direction will I need to take to get there?" This becomes your point of reference whenever you are embarking into the unknown.

The astronauts had Houston below them gathering data, giving feedback, and communicating how to adjust their booster engine thrusts. They were dealing with few constants: the moon was revolving, the earth was rotating, the space capsule was moving forward, the fuel was burning, and oxygen was being used up. In other words, everything was in an ongoing state of change. The basis for decision-making, however, was fixed: Where are we now? Where will that lead us? Where is the Moon? (Feedback). What shift in direction will lead us there? (Correction). Making the correction and getting back on course was then a cause for celebration.

Become an Observer

The purpose of feedback is to discover when you are headed in the wrong direction so that you can make corrections in your efforts. However, this can be seen only when you take on the role of an observer. It is very difficult to take a detached stance when you are either a participant in, or the leader of, the process. A lot of feedback was there from the early days of CSTN. People would say to Bill, "Why don't you just sell the training videos for companies to use?" But he considered this a superficial approach that had nothing to do with his vision for bringing planned, sustained, organizational change to American business. Yet in the long run, his passion for his dream blinded him from seeing certain signals. He could not hear what they "Houston" were saying and kept moving forward, ignoring/discarding the feedback around him.

Clarification Allows for Correction

For over a year, CSTN achieved an amazing level of productivity by producing and delivering *Programming for World-Class Performance* on a full-time, daily basis. This reinforced the belief that we could provide to the corporate world, via satellite, what it needed in order to compete globally and achieve world-class quality standards. The programming design was based on a level-three principle of adult learning, where new concepts or skills were introduced and implemented one idea at a time. The satellite technology made breakthrough material from some of the best minds in the world available to businesses and universities across the country. Then a member from each team receiving the training modules led the in-house implementation process.

During that period, however, it became clear that subscribing organizations were not capable of absorbing learning at the rate we were delivering it. To compensate, several clients began copying the programs for later use at their own convenience. Once on their shelves, these videotapes became part of their training department's domain. This was never our intention, and it was a violation of our client's contractual agreements. It also violated Bill's copyright agreements with the CSTN faculty.

Other design flaws emerged. We had developed an affiliate network consisting of some 40 established consultants and trainers who were to sell CSTN programming to their client base and support them in the implementation process. We totally overestimated their ability, time, or commitment to the level of deep organizational change that CSTN represented. Their loyalty to their own training programs or consulting services won out.

Although we quickly amassed an internationally renowned resource faculty and produced their material for satellite delivery, the faculty also found it difficult to actively support the network. Asking them to sell CSTN to their clients was like asking them to endorse and promote their own competitors.

In addition, potential CSTN clients with existing satellite systems had restrictive long-term agreements regarding the satellites they could access. In an effort to attract these companies to the CSTN programming and convert them to our full-time transponder, we expanded delivery of our programs to as many as four satellites. Too late, we discovered that the internal broadcast departments of these companies had a major investment in their own production facility, as well as a huge overhead. By using our programming, they would have eliminated the need for their existing departments and staff.

The Correction Process

Perhaps the true nature of correction needs some clarification. When correction is determined on the level of being wrong, it is very destructive and potentially devastating. That's because, when you think being off-plan is wrong, your effort is to get back on-plan and be right. This is where we tend to make the greatest errors and overreact to events.

If the astronauts had tried to get back on-plan every time they were off-plan, they would not have had enough fuel to get to the moon, much less to get safely back to earth. We would have had another episode of "lost in space." Many dreams get caught in this trap and become lost.

I once heard Bill say, "If people had not bought in so heavily to the concept of CSTN, I could have seen it sooner." The fact that there was so much buy-in kept us reinforced in the position that the concept was right. So we did everything in our power to keep it going.

For instance, at one point, when we both felt we were at the end of our ropes, we decided we might be missing a strong message—that we hadn't able to hear—to quit. Talking it over, we got down on our knees once more, ready to surrender our tenacious hold. The prayer went something like this:

Father, we have always felt your guiding hand in this dream and our fulfillment of it. You have sustained us, provided for us, and, in the process strengthened our family and our love. Thank you for these precious gifts. We are willing now to surrender the dream, and particularly our attachment to it, in lieu of Your will and Your highest purpose for our lives. Please give us the wisdom to discern what that is.

Early the next day, when one of our faculty members telephoned to say he had a check to give us for $10,000, we considered that to be the answer to our prayer. We were back in business! Typically, just when Bill would feel tired or discouraged, he would meet with a potential faculty member or CEO who was excited by his vision. This would renew his determination.

Determining Where You Are

As we went into our third year of satellite broadcast, the cost to operate continued to mount. The burn rate was approximately $100,000 per month beyond actual revenues. It became increasingly complex to integrate new clients while still supporting those who were two years into the programming. As we expanded globally with the live *Quality Imperative* teleconference series, time zone changes and language differences added to the complexity and costs of operations.

Although the quality and value of the programming was being validated, the feedback also included a high level of frustration from trying to schedule all employees into the daily and weekly programs. The bottom line of what a majority of the CSTN subscribers said was that, rather than having access to our faculty and programming through the satellite feed, they preferred the flexibility of a video resource library. They wanted to get it "off the shelf" rather than "off the satellite."

Bill knew this compromise approach would not fulfill his mission to bring about lasting organizational change. Training programs that lack total CEO participation and a continuous, team-based implementation process have a high failure rate. In spite of that, he arranged to fulfill the contract of each client in such a way that programming copyrights would not be violated.

We then made the final correction. In March 1992—exactly five years from CSTN's inception—the Corporate Satellite Television Network became The Learning Organization. The mission was fully intact; only the form had changed.

Although Bill and I, and countless others, had embraced a visionary concept with CSTN, it proved to be ahead of its time. Today, through new technology, small digital satellite dishes are readily available and affordable. Millions of businesses and homes are now able to access Direct TV at a greatly reduced cost compared to the analog technology available for our use ten years ago.

Bill continues to be contacted by individuals seeking ways to deliver distance learning through various media. In January 1999, we received a call asking how we might partner with an organization seeking to deliver business training programs to some 67,000 receive sites in China. Would we be interested in making our video-training library available for this purpose? The form or viability of any involvement on our part is still unknown. We are certain, however, given the way organizations work, that the only way for them to achieve lasting change is through knowledge transfer and becoming a learning organization.

The Completion Cycle

Since our business has come off satellite, our lives have been in an amazing process of completion, correction, and celebration. A quick reality check told us exactly where things stood. The licensing requirements that would have allowed me to immediately reestablish my private psychotherapy practice had changed. Having been out of direct consulting for eight years, it wasn't surprising to discover that all of our past clients had moved on. The Executive MBA curriculum we had developed and taught as Learning Laboratories through Brenau University had reverted to a standard MBA, and the dean with whom we had partnered was now retired.

So we started again from scratch, but with a quantitative difference—we were now $3 million dollars in debt. In addition, we had two young people to finish putting through college, and we still had a notice from the Resolution Trust Corporation (RTC) that our home was going to be repossessed. Talk about things requiring correction and completion!

Integrity versus Bankruptcy?

There is a place in countless people's lives loosely referred to as "where the rubber meets the road." I think of it as a place of nitty-gritty, look-yourself-in-the-eye, no-bull reality. It's a place of determination—for yourself—of the things you value, the kind of character you possess, and the kind of person you are. And that's the place where we found ourselves at this point in our lives. Bankruptcy was certainly one option, and during the early 1990's, a popular one.

I remember our children telling us that the entrepreneurial parents of a friend of theirs (they were considered quite well to do) were actually planning to max out all their credit cards and then file bankruptcy. What these people didn't understand, however, was that by not honoring their debts and by abusing their creditors, they violated two of the basic laws of life: the law of cause and effect (what you sow, you reap) and the law of giving and receiving (by giving joyfully that which you seek, you receive abundantly). Try it next month when you pay your bills—I derive great satisfaction from joyfully paying my bills because I know I am helping to keep a flow of abundance in our lives.

For us, it was a matter of personal integrity to honor our debts and repay all those who had believed in the dream. Bill made a commitment to pay back the entire $3,000,000 debt, and where appropriate, to provide greater value than received by offering his consulting services. This commitment included the $1,200,000 we had personally invested, the

$1,750,000 loaned to CSTN by banks, vendors, investors, or friends, and almost $50,000 of personal debt. He determined he would need to write $35,000 in checks per month for four years to retire these obligations, maintain integrity, and return the trust of every person who believed in us. This goal became a part of his personal purpose.

Celebration

Perhaps you are wondering how there would be anything to celebrate under the conditions I mention above. But the truth is that every correction or completion is cause for celebration! Celebration gives closure to phases or events in life, sustains an attitude of gratitude, and allows you to start anew.

We began tackling our personal debt by making an appointment with the Consumer Credit Counseling Service. This proved to be an excellent financial decision. Our counselor, Barbara Calhoun, was a tough, realistic, no-nonsense person who assisted us in setting up a repayment plan with 27 creditors. Gradually, over a three-year period, we paid each creditor back in full and became some of her star graduates. The day we made the final payment, Bill celebrated by buying a new sailboat to replace the one we previously sold in order to stay alive for one more month. We named it, "Razors Edge."

We did not, however, have the luxury of immediately restoring our good credit rating. It took seven years for us to have an R-1 "excellent credit" rating again.

We also negotiated refinancing of our home with the help of Newt Gingrich. Newt was then Speaker of the House and a congressman from Georgia. (He was a well-known history professor at the University of West Georgia during the time that our company Learning Laboratories conducted a Master degree program in organizational development there. We all became friends and were supportive of his first campaign for a seat in the House of Representatives.)

Everything came full-circle. After an initial phone conversation, Bill sent a letter to Newt asking for his assistance and direct intervention on our behalf. Newt sent a letter that got an immediate response from the RTC. All of a sudden, we were no longer a number to be dispensed with, but people of value. We had an appointment the next day with the head of the RTC in Atlanta, Randall Allford, who, it turned out, had been in one of Bill's seminars years before. We quickly set up a new mortgage repayment plan, and I was able to stop the frantic search for another place to live.

More Completions and Celebrations

By the end of 1997, except for the repayment to ourselves, we had personally repaid all investors, vendors, creditors, and friends, and fully retired the CSTN debt.

The repayment process we undertook became another test-by-fire of the concepts we had taught in the university program and in our consulting. It set the gyroscope for what our lives were to be about from then on—sharing what we discovered with others. Thus, for me, this book.

Life really does go on. I literally cannot tell from looking at my calendar where CSTN left off and The Learning Organization, Inc., began. A recent perusal of my appointment books from that time period reminded me how varied and exciting our life really was.

The Learning Organization's consulting services quickly expanded to Scandinavia and other international markets, allowing us the opportunity to travel across Europe and into northern Italy for our traditional family ski vacation. Other client relationships allowed our family to spend three weeks in Hong Kong and China, with a return visit now in the works.

Both Vail and Kord have graduated from private, well-respected colleges in the Northeast. (There is a wealth of financial resources available for your child's continuing education. I encourage you to investigate and use them.) They are each pursuing their individual entrepreneurial dreams. Vail is a talented young screenplay writer and independent filmmaker who presently resides in Los Angeles. While supporting himself as a popular and skilled teaching tennis pro, Kord has recently begun his first entrepreneurial business venture in Atlanta.

Every Breakdown Is a Potential Breakthrough

Bill was amazingly unaffected by the shift from satellite delivery because his dream for the possibilities for people in organizations was still intact. Unlike me, he was not attached to the form his vision took. Even though CSTN did not reach the staggering heights we had projected in our business plan, we are now helping the CEOs of other businesses to go beyond their highest aspirations, and we are benefiting in direct proportion to their success.

Under the Learning Organization umbrella, Bill has taken what CSTN was designed to achieve and transformed it into a hands-on organizational model based on the principles and tools we discovered during the past thirty years. This model, known as the CEO Alliance, is a forum that allows CEOs of rapid-growth companies to band together to grow their businesses. Almost every lesson we learned in CSTN has been powerfully implemented to change the way these organizations operate and the way their CEOs lead their organizations. Bill's upcoming book, *Controlling Your Organizational Destiny by Creating the Future*, chronicles these successes.

I sit here today and am amazed by what I observe in our lives. Every breakdown truly contains the potential for a breakthrough! Each breakthrough is an opportunity for growth and celebration. I urge you to celebrate every completion and each correction! As you discover the principles that determine success, and know to Whom and on what to place your faith, you will find deeper levels of meaning in all that you do.

The Celebration of Life

The discovery of meaning is the celebration of life. Meaning results from knowing that the choices you make are based on fundamental truths. It results from having all your actions stem from your personal purpose. This is where you come from. Where you come from is always where you will end up. In a sense, the search is over the moment you know the Source from which you come. This is the Source of all faith. Without knowing this, there is no real faith.

The process of discovery and growth, however, is just begun. It accelerates by choosing to share it. Sharing is celebration. It means being connected to all those around you in a manner that continuously increases your contribution to them. Remember that celebration is in direct proportion to your degree of contribution. In this environment of contribution, sharing, and growth, you will always find that energy and creativity abound. Resources suddenly appear and are there to serve you. You access them out of your vision and your desire to serve others.

I applaud you for your willingness to embrace the unknown and utilize the wealth of resources that are already available to aid you in the fulfillment of your dream. I encourage each one of you to keep stepping forward in faith, guided by your Vision and armed with your commitment to a great purpose. Be assured that the ancient words of the great leader Moses (Deuteronomy 31:8) to his successor, Joshua, are just as true this day for you: "The Lord himself goes before you and will be with you; he will never leave you nor forsake you. Do not be afraid; do not be discouraged."

The Heritage

Writing this book has taught me a great deal. It has clarified what works and what does not. It has reminded me of who I am and what each of us is capable of mastering. It has revealed the power of a dream and the unlimited resources available in the pursuit of that dream. We are shaped by our dreams. We become them, and they become us. And in the process, they leave a heritage—an indelible imprint on whom we have become. The bigger the dream, the better we are able to discover what we have or have not become.

Though your dream may die or take a form other than you originally envisioned, having pursued it will leave you with an enormous legacy. This legacy will live on in your values and the way you choose to live your life. In the aftermath of any challenging experience or loss, it is helpful to determine what you have gained or learned in the process. In retrospect, I believe the Schwarz family heritage includes the following

221

(with this example, I encourage you to create your own family heritage by writing down incidents that fall into these categories):

Patience. We learned to wait expectantly. With the realization that things take longer than planned, and that unplanned things happen suddenly (and not always according to our plans), we developed the capacity for calm endurance.

Grace. We came to accept the grace of God into our daily lives. We developed the calm assurance that a Higher Wisdom was at work and that those unseen resources would continue to appear and to sustain us.

Emotional Detachment. We learned to relinquish our expectations of others in order to be happy, and not to rely on material things for ego satisfaction or a definition of personal value.

Compassion. The pain each of us has encountered in the pursuit of our dreams enables us to feel more deeply the challenges, isolation, and hurt of others.

Tenacity. Not only have we dreamed our dreams, but we have held firmly to them and to each other beyond all odds. Tenacity and persistence made the difference between having luck (good fortune) and pluck (a resourceful, courageous spirit).

Humility. Through loss, setbacks, and constant delays, we observed how little ability we had to personally control people, timetables, or outcomes. We discovered how dependent we were on the grace of God and the goodness of others.

Renewed Faith in God. Many times we were driven to our knees by the certainty that we could not get through another day on our own wisdom and strength alone. Out of that surrender, we found strength to let go of our fear and the will to be healed of the enormous toll that the accumulated stress had taken on our family unity and marriage.

Comfort in Sorrows. With the passing of loved ones who suffered the indignities of old age, painful illnesses, and the loss of control over their normal bodily functions, we were reminded that health is precious, life is fleeting, and death is seldom proud. We learned to surrender our selfish desires for those things to the all-knowing Power that could best discern their highest good.

Triumph over Fears. Life on the edge is no longer terrifying or debilitating. The unknown has become just the unknown—part of the adventure of life.

One essential thing I think we all fail to recognize and give ourselves credit for is that we are always putting ourselves into learning situations that are necessary for our next stage of contribution or growth. The great deception we perpetuate is the thought that the circumstances of life—people, things, conditions, or natural phenomena—are the cause of our suffering, misery, and misfortune. This saps our energy and distorts everything around us. When we can see things from the higher awareness of personal responsibility and creative power, no situation needs to be considered a danger or an emotional threat.

We are all blessed. We all experience grace in our lives. Resources abound and are there to serve us—suddenly appearing literally from nowhere. We access them out of our vision and our commitment to serving others. You can create serenity, happiness, and an inner security for living a fulfilled and purposeful life. My desire is to enable individuals, families, and businesses to sustain their dreams and enlarge their ability to focus on the big picture. Remember—you don't have to do it alone.

About

Lauren Black Schwarz

LAUREN BLACK SCHWARZ IS a teacher, consultant, speaker, and co-founder with her husband, William Schwarz, of Learning Laboratories, Inc., CSTN, The Learning Organization, and the CEO Alliance. For many years she worked with hundreds of individuals, couples, and groups as a psychotherapist and a principal of the Life Management Center, before stepping away to partner with her husband as they launched the global business concept described in this book. She holds a double Masters Degree in Psychology and Organizational Development and has taught university courses on Change Management, Communication, and Leadership Development. She and her husband, Bill, have raised two entrepreneurial children, Vail and Kord.

The Learning Organization, Inc.

FOUNDED AS LEARNING LABORATORIES, in 1972, The Learning Organization is an international consulting firm which specializes in implementing optimum-growth strategies. TLO works with executive teams committed to organizational excellence through the implementation of learning organization principles and practices and the application of systems-thinking concepts.

The vision of The Learning Organization is for its clients to be able to create their future and control their destiny through shared values and inspired vision. To realize its mission TLO has developed a powerful and unique process of change, known as the CEO Alliance. The CEO Alliance partners with CEO's to design and develop their core strategies and capabilities.

The Learning Organization is Located at 1641 Doncaster Dr. NE, Atlanta, GA 30309. The Learning Organization can be contacted at 1-800-875-4180 or faxed at 1-404-875-4452.